I Have, Who Has?

LANGUAGE ARTS

3–4

Written by
Trisha Callella

Editor: Carla Hamaguchi
Cover Illustrator: Corbin Hillam
Production: Moonhee Pak and Carrie Rickmond
Designer: Moonhee Pak
Art Director: Tom Cochrane

Reprinted 2008

Table of Contents

Introduction

I HAVE, WHO HAS is a series of books that provide interactive group activities. The activities consist of game cards that students read and interactively answer. Each card game consists of 40 cards. The game starts when a student reads the first card. The student who has the card with the answer reads his or her card. The game continues in this manner until the last card is read. The last card's question "loops" back to the first card.

This book provides a fun, interactive way for students to practice various language arts skills. This resource includes over 35 card games that will improve students' listening skills and teach standards-based skills and strategies. The skills covered include:

- Synonyms
- Antonyms
- Homophones
- Compound Words
- Grammar
- Prefixes and Suffixes
- Greek and Latin Roots
- Syllabication
- Rhyming Words
- Multiple-Meaning Words
- Context Clues
- Fact or Opinion
- Vocabulary

Each game also features an active listening and enrichment activity. This component gives students practice in active listening and extends their learning to the application level.

Even better is the fact that there is hardly any prep work required to start these games in your class. Simply make copies of the game cards, cut them apart, and you are ready to go! These engaging games will keep students entertained as they are learning valuable language arts skills.

Getting Started

ORGANIZATION

There are 40 reproducible cards for each game. The cards are arranged in columns (top to bottom) in the order they will be read by the class. A reproducible active listening and enrichment page follows every set of game cards. The interactive card games for reviewing skills and strategies can be used alone or in conjunction with this reproducible page to have students practice active listening, increase active participation, provide enrichment, and extend and transfer the learning and accountability of each student.

INSTRUCTIONS FOR I HAVE, WHO HAS GAME CARDS

1) Photocopy two sets of the game cards. (Each game has four pages of 10 cards each.)

2) Cut apart one set of game cards. Mix up the cards. Pass out at least one card to each student. (There are 40 cards to accommodate large class sizes. If your class size is less than 40, then some students will have two cards. The important thing is that every student has at least one card.)

3) Keep one copy of the game cards as your reference to the correct order. The cards are printed in order in columns from top to bottom and left to right.

4) Have the student with the first game card begin the game by saying *I have the first card. Who has . . . ?* As each student reads a card, monitor your copy to make sure students are reading the cards in the correct order. If students correctly matched each card, then the last card read will "loop" back to the first card.

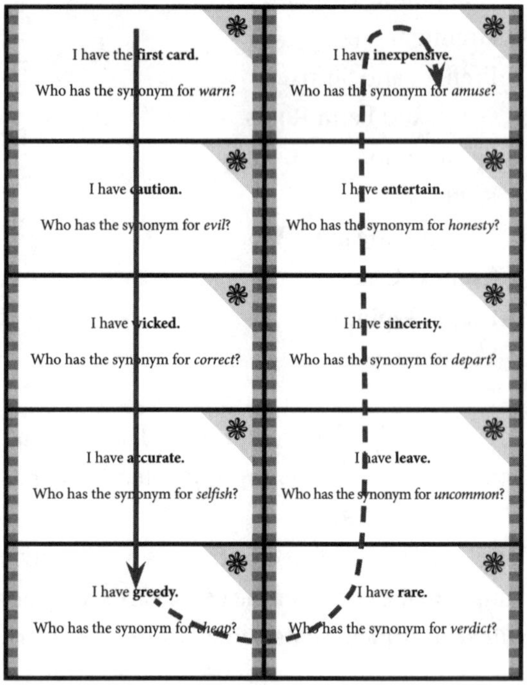

INSTRUCTIONS FOR ACTIVE LISTENING & ENRICHMENT PAGE

1) This page is optional and is not necessary to play the game.

2) Copy one page for each student or pair of students.

3) Make sure each student has a light-colored crayon or highlighter (not a marker or pencil) to color over the correct boxes as they are read.

4) As each matching card is read, provide time for students to highlight or lightly color in the correct box. If the game is slow for a particular class, two children can help each other with one reproducible page.

5) After the last card is read ("Who has the first card?"), ask students to uncover the hidden text (e.g., riddle, proverb) by reading the text in all the boxes they did not highlight or color. Have them read from top to bottom and from left to right on the grid. Then, have them answer the extension questions at the bottom of the page.

6) Use the answer key on pages 196–204 to check students' answers.

WHAT TO WATCH FOR

1) Students who have difficulty locating the correct boxes on the active listening and enrichment page after the first game (establish familiarity with the format) may have visual discrimination difficulties.

2) Students who have difficulty reading their card at the correct time may have difficulties with attention, hearing, active listening, or the concepts being reinforced.

VARIATIONS

Timed Version

1) Follow the instructions to prepare the game cards so that each student has at least one. Play without the reproducible page. Tell students that they will play the game twice. Challenge them to beat their time in the second round.

2) Have students play the same game again the next day. Can they beat their time again? Remember to mix up the cards and redistribute them before each game.

3) The more students play, the better they will understand the concepts covered in each game. They will also develop stronger phrasing and fluency in reading.

Small Groups

1) Photocopy one set of game cards (four pages, 40 cards total) for each small group. Play without the reproducible page.

2) Cut apart the cards, mix them up, and give a set to each group.

3) Have each group play. You can time the groups to encourage them to pay close attention, read quickly, and stay on task. Which group is the fastest?

4) By playing in smaller groups, each student has more cards. This raises the individual accountability, activity, time on task, and reinforcement opportunities per student.

Synonyms 1

I have the **first card**.

Who has the synonym for *end*?

I have **annoy**.

Who has the synonym for *ask*?

I have **conclude**.

Who has the synonym for *viewpoint*?

I have **request**.

Who has the synonym for *convince*?

I have **opinion**.

Who has the synonym for *correct*?

I have **persuade**.

Who has the synonym for *insist*?

I have **accurate**.

Who has the synonym for *thoughts*?

I have **demand**.

Who has the synonym for *begin*?

I have **ideas**.

Who has the synonym for *bother*?

I have **start**.

Who has the synonym for *hesitate*?

Synonyms 1

I have **pause**.

Who has the synonym for *respond*?

I have **tension**.

Who has the synonym for *brief*?

I have **answer**.

Who has the synonym for *change*?

I have **short**.

Who has the synonym for *fake*?

I have **alter**.

Who has the synonym for *oath*?

I have **artificial**.

Who has the synonym for *ruined*?

I have **pledge**.

Who has the synonym for *solution*?

I have **destroyed**.

Who has the synonym for *happy*?

I have **result**.

Who has the synonym for *conflict*?

I have **glad**.

Who has the synonym for *ill*?

Synonyms 1

I have **sick**.

Who has the synonym for *buy*?

I have **clean**.

Who has the synonym for *hope*?

I have **purchase**.

Who has the synonym for *funny*?

I have **wish**.

Who has the synonym for *gorgeous*?

I have **humorous**.

Who has the synonym for *exit*?

I have **pretty**.

Who has the synonym for *speedy*?

I have **leave**.

Who has the synonym for *easy*?

I have **quick**.

Who has the synonym for *wealthy*?

I have **simple**.

Who has the synonym for *tidy*?

I have **rich**.

Who has the synonym for *teach*?

Synonyms 1

I have **educate**.

Who has the synonym for *achieve*?

I have **relaxed**.

Who has the synonym for *frightening*?

I have **accomplish**.

Who has the synonym for *enormous*?

I have **fearsome**.

Who has the synonym for *thoughtful*?

I have **gigantic**.

Who has the synonym for *nearby*?

I have **considerate**.

Who has the synonym for *gift*?

I have **close**.

Who has the synonym for *risky*?

I have **present**.

Who has the synonym for *remember*?

I have **dangerous**.

Who has the synonym for *calm*?

I have **recall**.

Who has the first card?

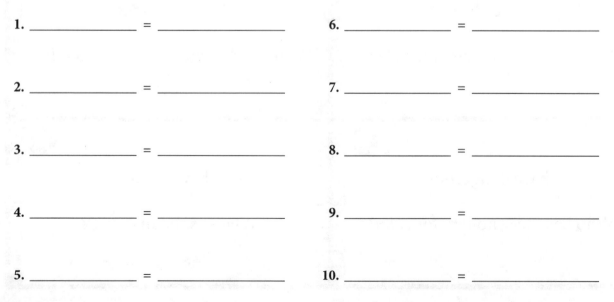

Synonyms 1

Follow the path by highlighting the answers as your classmates identify them.

START *	COMPANION	PRESENT	**FINISH** * RECALL	DIFFICULT
CONCLUDE	FEARSOME	CONSIDERATE	GIGANTIC	ACCOMPLISH
OPINION	RELAXED	DANGEROUS	CLOSE	EDUCATE
ACCURATE	IDEAS	BRAVE	ENORMOUS	RICH
REQUEST	ANNOY	PITY	PRETTY	QUICK
PERSUADE	AID	CLEAN	WISH	SLOW
DEMAND	START	SIMPLE	LEAVE	HUMOROUS
ANSWER	PAUSE	RUSH	ARRIVE	PURCHASE
ALTER	COLLECT	SHORT	ARTIFICIAL	SICK
PLEDGE	RESULT	TENSION	DESTROYED	GLAD

Now write the words that are **not** highlighted above on the lines below. Write a synonym for each word.

1. ________________ = ____________________ **6.** ________________ = ____________________

2. ________________ = ____________________ **7.** ________________ = ____________________

3. ________________ = ____________________ **8.** ________________ = ____________________

4. ________________ = ____________________ **9.** ________________ = ____________________

5. ________________ = ____________________ **10.** ________________ = ____________________

Synonyms 2

I have the **first card**.

Who has the synonym for *warn*?

I have **inexpensive**.

Who has the synonym for *amuse*?

I have **caution**.

Who has the synonym for *evil*?

I have **entertain**.

Who has the synonym for *honesty*?

I have **wicked**.

Who has the synonym for *correct*?

I have **sincerity**.

Who has the synonym for *depart*?

I have **accurate**.

Who has the synonym for *selfish*?

I have **leave**.

Who has the synonym for *uncommon*?

I have **greedy**.

Who has the synonym for *cheap*?

I have **rare**.

Who has the synonym for *verdict*?

Synonyms 2

I have **judgment**.

Who has the synonym for *absent*?

I have **doubt**.

Who has the synonym for *spotless*?

I have **gone**.

Who has the synonym for *start*?

I have **clean**.

Who has the synonym for *generous*?

I have **begin**.

Who has the synonym for *fake*?

I have **giving**.

Who has the synonym for *rip*?

I have **artificial**.

Who has the synonym for *well-planned*?

I have **tear**.

Who has the synonym for *prize*?

I have **organized**.

Who has the synonym for *disbelieve*?

I have **award**.

Who has the synonym for *wrongful*?

Synonyms 2

I have **unjust**.

Who has the synonym for *poisonous*?

I have **tremble**.

Who has the synonym for *gather*?

I have **toxic**.

Who has the synonym for *build*?

I have **collect**.

Who has the synonym for *help*?

I have **construct**.

Who has the synonym for *late*?

I have **assist**.

Who has the synonym for *supplies*?

I have **tardy**.

Who has the synonym for *talk*?

I have **materials**.

Who has the synonym for *predict*?

I have **speak**.

Who has the synonym for *shake*?

I have **foretell**.

Who has the synonym for *tiny*?

Synonyms 2

I have **petite**. Who has the synonym for *piece*?	I have **tough**. Who has the synonym for *promise*?
I have **section**. Who has the synonym for *smart*?	I have **vow**. Who has the synonym for *known*?
I have **intelligent**. Who has the synonym for *smash*?	I have **familiar**. Who has the synonym for *human*?
I have **crush**. Who has the synonym for *renter*?	I have **person**. Who has the synonym for *observe*?
I have **tenant**. Who has the synonym for *difficult*?	I have **notice**. Who has the first card?

Synonyms 2

Fill in the missing letters of the synonyms as your classmates identify them. Start at the arrow and go from left to right and top to bottom.

→ _ A U _ I O _	_ I _ _ E _	A _ _ U _ A _ _	_ _ E E _ _
_ _ E X _ E _ S _ V _	_ N _ E _ T A _ _	_ I _ _ E _ I _ _	_ E A _ _
_ _ R _	_ U D _ _ E _ _	_ _ N _	_ E _ I _
A _ _ I _ I C I A _	_ R _ A _ I _ E _	_ O U B _	_ _ E A _
_ I _ I _ _	_ E A _	A _ A _ _	U _ _ _ _ T
_ O X _ _	_ O _ _ _ _ U _ _	_ A _ _ _	_ _ E A _
_ _ E _ _ _ E	_ O _ _ E _ _	A _ _ I _ _	_ A _ E _ I A _ _
_ O _ E _ E _ _	_ E _ I _ E	_ E _ _ I _ _	I _ _ E _ _ I _ E _ _
_ _ U _ _	_ E _ A _ _	_ O U _ _	_ O _
_ A _ I _ I A _	_ E _ _ O _	_ O _ I _ E	SMART
A	**B**	**C**	**D**

List the words from Column C. Then write a new synonym for each word.

1. ________________ = ____________________   6. ________________ = ____________________

2. ________________ = ____________________   7. ________________ = ____________________

3. ________________ = ____________________   8. ________________ = ____________________

4. ________________ = ____________________   9. ________________ = ____________________

5. ________________ = ____________________   10. ________________ = ____________________

Synonyms 3

I have the **first card**.

Who has the synonym for *solution*?

I have **stare**.

Who has the synonym for *toss*?

I have **answer**.

Who has the synonym for *big*?

I have **throw**.

Who has the synonym for *hide*?

I have **large**.

Who has the synonym for *destroy*?

I have **conceal**.

Who has the synonym for *nap*?

I have **ruin**.

Who has the synonym for *silly*?

I have **snooze**.

Who has the synonym for *design*?

I have **ridiculous**.

Who has the synonym for *gaze*?

I have **create**.

Who has the synonym for *pull*?

Synonyms 3

I have **tow**.

Who has the synonym for *angry*?

I have **describe**.

Who has the synonym for *powerful*?

I have **upset**.

Who has the synonym for *chair*?

I have **strong**.

Who has the synonym for *certainly*?

I have **seat**.

Who has the synonym for *own*?

I have **definitely**.

Who has the synonym for *untrue*?

I have **possess**.

Who has the synonym for *want*?

I have **false**.

Who has the synonym for *pretty*?

I have **desire**.

Who has the synonym for *explain*?

I have **attractive**.

Who has the synonym for *change*?

Synonyms 3

I have **revise**.

Who has the synonym for *damaged*?

I have **astonished**.

Who has the synonym for *shy*?

I have **harmed**.

Who has the synonym for *path*?

I have **bashful**.

Who has the synonym for *hopeful*?

I have **trail**.

Who has the synonym for *admire*?

I have **optimistic**.

Who has the synonym for *unkind*?

I have **respect**.

Who has the synonym for *modern*?

I have **cruel**.

Who has the synonym for *authentic*?

I have **current**.

Who has the synonym for *shocked*?

I have **genuine**.

Who has the synonym for *defeat?*

Synonyms 3

I have **conquer**.

Who has the synonym for *costly*?

I have **imitate**.

Who has the synonym for *depart*?

I have **expensive**.

Who has the synonym for *forecast*?

I have **leave**.

Who has the synonym for *bucket*?

I have **predict**.

Who has the synonym for *hollow*?

I have **pail**.

Who has the synonym for *clap*?

I have **empty**.

Who has the synonym for *silent*?

I have **applaud**.

Who has the synonym for *prevent*?

I have **quiet**.

Who has the synonym for *mimic*?

I have **stop**.

Who has the first card?

Synonyms 3

Follow the path by highlighting the answers as your classmates identify them.

Why did the computer go to the doctor?

BECAUSE	TRAIL	RESPECT	BASHFUL	OPTIMISTIC
CUTE	HARMED	CURRENT	ASTONISHED	CRUEL
ATTRACTIVE	REVISE	IT	CONQUER	GENUINE
FALSE	POSSESS	SEAT	EXPENSIVE	PREDICT
DEFINITELY	DESIRE	UPSET	HAPPY	EMPTY
STRONG	DESCRIBE	TOW	IMITATE	QUIET
HAD	HELPFUL	CREATE	LEAVE	PAIL
LARGE	RUIN	SNOOZE	A	APPLAUD
ANSWER	RIDICULOUS	CONCEAL	CLEAN	**FINISH** * STOP
START *	STARE	THROW	VIRUS	SMART

Start at the top left box of the chart and circle every other word that is **not** highlighted. Write the circled words in order below to solve the riddle.

__________ __________ __________ __________ __________!

Write the words that are **not** circled or highlighted. Write a synonym for each word.

1. __________ = __________
2. __________ = __________
3. __________ = __________
4. __________ = __________
5. __________ = __________

Synonyms 4

I have the **first card**.

Who has the synonym for *shut*?

I have **grateful**.

Who has the synonym for *shout*?

I have **close**.

Who has the synonym for *find*?

I have **yell**.

Who has the synonym for *tired*?

I have **discover**.

Who has the synonym for *scared*?

I have **exhausted**.

Who has the synonym for *foolish*?

I have **afraid**.

Who has the synonym for *fast*?

I have **silly**.

Who has the synonym for *bag*?

I have **rapid**.

Who has the synonym for *thankful*?

I have **sack**.

Who has the synonym for *shine*?

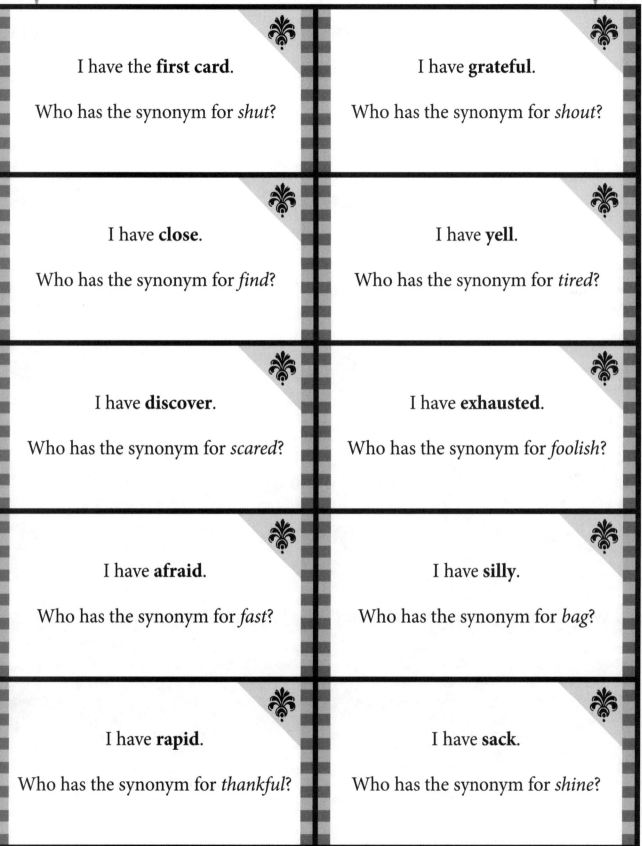

Synonyms 4

I have **polish**.

Who has the synonym for *fix*?

I have **select**.

Who has the synonym for *divide*?

I have **repair**.

Who has the synonym for *unlike*?

I have **split**.

Who has the synonym for *sure*?

I have **different**.

Who has the synonym for *far*?

I have **positive**.

Who has the synonym for *rescue*?

I have **distant**.

Who has the synonym for *assistant*?

I have **save**.

Who has the synonym for *examine*?

I have **helper**.

Who has the synonym for *pick*?

I have **inspect**.

Who has the synonym for *melt*?

Synonyms 4

I have **thaw**.

Who has the synonym for *view*?

I have **finish**.

Who has the synonym for *easy*?

I have **observe**.

Who has the synonym for *deadly*?

I have **simple**.

Who has the synonym for *blame*?

I have **lethal**.

Who has the synonym for *dirty*?

I have **accuse**.

Who has the synonym for *follow*?

I have **grimy**.

Who has the synonym for *hire*?

I have **pursue**.

Who has the synonym for *allow*?

I have **employ**.

Who has the synonym for *complete*?

I have **permit**.

Who has the synonym for *unimportant*?

Synonyms 4

I have **petty**.

Who has the synonym for *edge*?

I have **numerous**.

Who has the synonym for *remain*?

I have **rim**.

Who has the synonym for *demand*?

I have **stay**.

Who has the synonym for *example*?

I have **insist**.

Who has the synonym for *inside*?

I have **sample**.

Who has the synonym for *supper*?

I have **indoors**.

Who has the synonym for *cost*?

I have **dinner**.

Who has the synonym for *enemy*?

I have **expense**.

Who has the synonym for *many*?

I have **foe**.

Who has the first card?

Synonyms 4

As your classmates identify the answers, highlight the letters that spell each synonym. Each new word is near the previous word. Words do not share letters and do not go backwards or diagonally. Clue: The first word is in the second row.

A	E	E	M	P	L	O	Y	F	I	N	I	S	H	I	N	D	O	O	R	S
G	R	I	M	Y	C	L	O	S	E	D	S	P	R	I	M	U	U	W	E	C
L	E	T	H	A	L	A	E	I	O	I	I	E	U	I	L	N	O	O	X	A
E	O	O	B	S	E	R	V	E	A	S	M	T	O	N	A	O	I	R	P	S
T	H	A	W	M	E	S	S	Y	I	C	P	T	I	S	T	R	E	T	E	H
P	O	O	I	N	S	P	E	C	T	O	L	Y	P	I	E	G	A	H	N	N
O	S	A	V	E	O	D	A	U	I	V	E	E	E	S	G	A	E	W	S	U
S	T	H	A	S	I	I	I	S	E	E	A	P	R	T	R	N	X	H	E	M
I	A	E	I	E	O	F	L	E	A	R	C	U	M	O	A	I	H	I	E	E
T	R	L	I	L	E	F	L	F	F	A	C	R	I	O	T	Z	A	L	A	R
I	D	P	O	E	O	E	I	U	R	E	U	S	T	A	E	E	U	E	S	O
V	Y	E	A	C	O	R	R	L	A	I	S	U	E	E	F	D	S	U	A	U
E	U	R	A	T	A	E	E	U	I	O	E	E	E	I	U	O	T	O	M	S
S	P	L	I	T	I	N	P	A	D	R	A	P	I	D	L	A	E	I	P	S
M	O	N	E	Y	E	T	A	E	A	E	I	O	Y	E	L	L	D	E	L	T
D	I	S	T	A	N	T	I	S	M	A	R	T	S	I	L	L	Y	A	E	A
C	L	E	V	E	R	U	R	O	S	A	C	K	A	D	I	N	N	E	R	Y
U	O	A	I	P	O	L	I	S	H	A	A	A	F	O	E	S	I	C	K	A

Match the synonyms below and then find them in the areas of the word search you did **not** highlight.

1. ______ useful

2. ______ smart

3. ______ sick

4. ______ late

5. ______ messy

6. ______ cash

a. tardy

b. unorganized

c. worthwhile

d. money

e. clever

f. ill

HINT: If you did everything correctly, all the remaining letters are vowels.

Antonyms 1

I have the **first card**.

Who has the antonym for *silent*?

I have **end**.

Who has the antonym for *include*?

I have **noisy**.

Who has the antonym for *proud*?

I have **omit**.

Who has the antonym for *spend*?

I have **ashamed**.

Who has the antonym for *success*?

I have **save**.

Who has the antonym for *friendly*?

I have **failure**.

Who has the antonym for *lend*?

I have **mean**.

Who has the antonym for *misplace*?

I have **borrow**.

Who has the antonym for *begin*?

I have **locate**.

Who has the antonym for *gain*?

Antonyms 1

I have **lose**.

Who has the antonym for *enter*?

I have **lower**.

Who has the antonym for *admit*?

I have **exit**.

Who has the antonym for *purchase*?

I have **deny**.

Who has the antonym for *fact*?

I have **sell**.

Who has the antonym for *argue*?

I have **opinion**.

Who has the antonym for *ask*?

I have **agree**.

Who has the antonym for *depart*?

I have **answer**.

Who has the antonym for *release*?

I have **arrive**.

Who has the antonym for *raise*?

I have **trap**.

Who has the antonym for *unlucky*?

Antonyms 1

I have **fortunate**.

Who has the antonym for *graceful*?

I have **healthy**.

Who has the antonym for *cause*?

I have **clumsy**.

Who has the antonym for *increase*?

I have **effect**.

Who has the antonym for *behind*?

I have **decrease**.

Who has the antonym for *moist*?

I have **ahead**.

Who has the antonym for *public*?

I have **dry**.

Who has the antonym for *messy*?

I have **private**.

Who has the antonym for *conceal*?

I have **organized**.

Who has the antonym for *diseased*?

I have **reveal**.

Who has the antonym for *straight*?

Antonyms 1

I have **curved**.

Who has the antonym for *risky*?

I have **repair**.

Who has the antonym for *exciting*?

I have **safe**.

Who has the antonym for *joined*?

I have **boring**.

Who has the antonym for *near*?

I have **separate**.

Who has the antonym for *expert*?

I have **distant**.

Who has the antonym for *nonfiction*?

I have **novice**.

Who has the antonym for *punish*?

I have **fiction**.

Who has the antonym for *mature*?

I have **reward**.

Who has the antonym for *damage*?

I have **immature**.

Who has the first card?

Antonyms 1

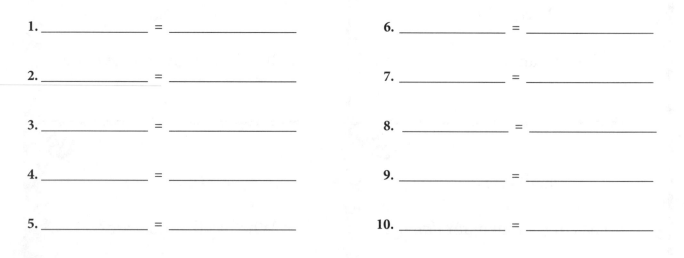

Follow the path by highlighting the answers as your classmates identify them.

BORING	DISTANT	FICTION	**FINISH** * IMMATURE	COMICAL
REPAIR	DEADLY	LEAVE	DIVIDE	GLOSSY
REWARD	NOVICE	SEPARATE	REVEAL	PRIVATE
INITIAL	PEACEFUL	SAFE	CURVED	AHEAD
START *	NOISY	ASHAMED	FAILURE	EFFECT
LOCATE	MEAN	SAVE	BORROW	HEALTHY
LOSE	SIMPLE	OMIT	END	ORGANIZED
EXIT	SUCCEED	OPINION	ANSWER	DRY
SELL	AGREE	DENY	TRAP	DECREASE
ROUGH	ARRIVE	LOWER	FORTUNATE	CLUMSY

Now write the words that are **not** highlighted above on the lines below. Write an antonym for each word.

1. ______________ = ________________
2. ______________ = ________________
3. ______________ = ________________
4. ______________ = ________________
5. ______________ = ________________
6. ______________ = ________________
7. ______________ = ________________
8. ______________ = ________________
9. ______________ = ________________
10. ______________ = ________________

Antonyms 2

I have the **first card.**

Who has the antonym for *then*?

I have **inside**.

Who has the antonym for *teacher*?

I have **now**.

Who has the antonym for *past*?

I have **student**.

Who has the antonym for *loyal*?

I have **future**.

Who has the antonym for *whisper*?

I have **disloyal**.

Who has the antonym for *send*?

I have **shout**.

Who has the antonym for *protect*?

I have **receive**.

Who has the antonym for *famous*?

I have **endanger**.

Who has the antonym for *outside*?

I have **unknown**.

Who has the antonym for *find*?

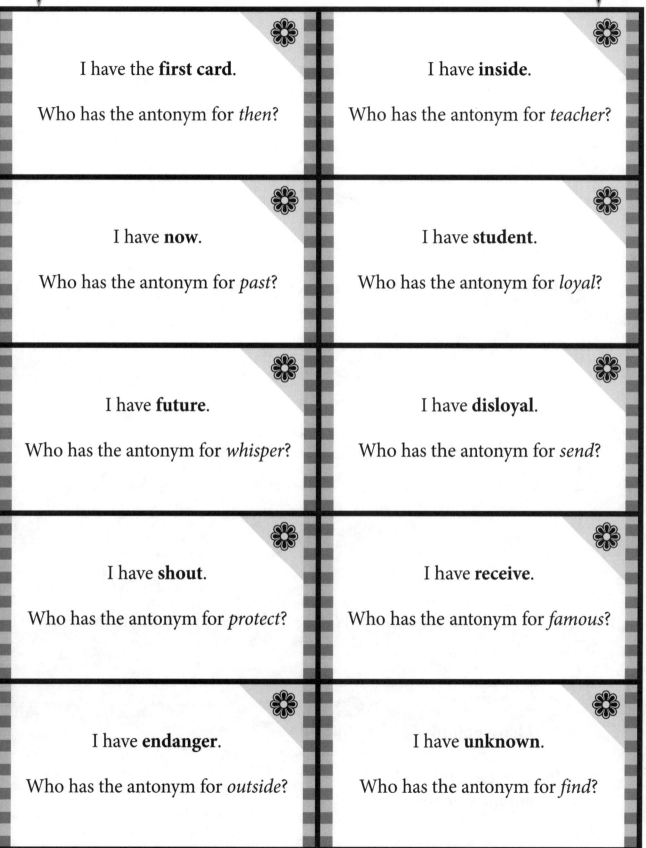

Antonyms 2

I have **misplace**. Who has the antonym for *follow*?	I have **comprehend**. Who has the antonym for *modern*?
I have **lead**. Who has the antonym for *bitter*?	I have **ancient**. Who has the antonym for *remember*?
I have **sweet**. Who has the antonym for *interior*?	I have **forget**. Who has the antonym for *late*?
I have **exterior**. Who has the antonym for *somebody*?	I have **prompt**. Who has the antonym for *wealth*?
I have **nobody**. Who has the antonym for *misunderstand*?	I have **poverty**. Who has the antonym for *common*?

Antonyms 2

I have **unique**.

Who has the antonym for *thin*?

I have **ignore**.

Who has the antonym for *absent*?

I have **thick**.

Who has the antonym for *morning*?

I have **present**.

Who has the antonym for *hid*?

I have **evening**.

Who has the antonym for *sure*?

I have **revealed**.

Who has the antonym for *continue*?

I have **uncertain**.

Who has the antonym for *normal*?

I have **cease**.

Who has the antonym for *innocent*?

I have **abnormal**.

Who has the antonym for *disturb*?

I have **guilty**.

Who has the antonym for *sturdy*?

Antonyms 2

I have **feeble**.

Who has the antonym for *pure*?

I have **expert**.

Who has the antonym for *accept*?

I have **tainted**.

Who has the antonym for *mild*?

I have **reject**.

Who has the antonym for *portion*?

I have **harsh**.

Who has the antonym for *near*?

I have **whole**.

Who has the antonym for *insult*?

I have **distant**.

Who has the antonym for *confuse*?

I have **compliment**.

Who has the antonym for *boastful*?

I have **clarify**.

Who has the antonym for *amateur*?

I have **humble**.

Who has the first card?

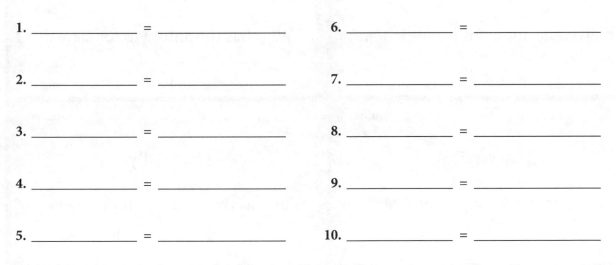

Antonyms 2

Fill in the missing letters of the antonyms as your classmates identify them. Start at the arrow and go from left to right and top to bottom.

→	_O_	_U_U_E	__OU_
E_____E_	_____E	__U_E__	_I__OY__
_E_EI__	__K__W_	_I___A__	_EA_
__E__	___E_I__	___O__	_O___E_E__
A__IE__	____E_	__O__T	_O_E__Y
U_I__E	__I__	__E____	__CE__AI_
A_______	_G_O__	__E_E__	___EA___
_EA__	_UI___	__E___	_AI____
_A___	_I__A__	__A___Y	___E__
__J___	W____	_O___I____	_U____
A	**B**	**C**	**D**

List the words from Column B. Then write a new antonym for each word.

1. ______________ = ______________
2. ______________ = ______________
3. ______________ = ______________
4. ______________ = ______________
5. ______________ = ______________
6. ______________ = ______________
7. ______________ = ______________
8. ______________ = ______________
9. ______________ = ______________
10. ______________ = ______________

Antonyms 3

I have the **first card**.

Who has the antonym for *finished*?

I have **pollute**.

Who has the antonym for *brave*?

I have **incomplete**.

Who has the antonym for *above*?

I have **cowardly**.

Who has the antonym for *drop*?

I have **below**.

Who has the antonym for *quit*?

I have **catch**.

Who has the antonym for *exact*?

I have **persevere**.

Who has the antonym for *horizontal*?

I have **approximate**.

Who has the antonym for *clever*?

I have **vertical**.

Who has the antonym for *clean*?

I have **silly**.

Who has the antonym for *authentic*?

Antonyms 3

I have **counterfeit**.

Who has the antonym for *attract*?

I have **shrink**.

Who has the antonym for *useless*?

I have **repel**.

Who has the antonym for *irritate*?

I have **useful**.

Who has the antonym for *difficult*?

I have **soothe**.

Who has the antonym for *joy*?

I have **easy**.

Who has the antonym for *harmless*?

I have **sadness**.

Who has the antonym for *sort*?

I have **deadly**.

Who has the antonym for *addition*?

I have **blend**.

Who has the antonym for *grow*?

I have **subtraction**.

Who has the antonym for *busy*?

Antonyms 3

I have **inactive**.

Who has the antonym for *youthful*?

I have **counterclockwise**.

Who has the antonym for *rugged*?

I have **aged**.

Who has the antonym for *caught*?

I have **smooth**.

Who has the antonym for *fresh*?

I have **freed**.

Who has the antonym for *meet*?

I have **stale**.

Who has the antonym for *beautiful*?

I have **avoid**.

Who has the antonym for *nightfall*?

I have **ugly**.

Who has the antonym for *stretch*?

I have **dawn**.

Who has the antonym for *clockwise*?

I have **contract**.

Who has the antonym for *omit*?

Antonyms 3

I have **include**.

Who has the antonym for *minimum*?

I have **reveal**.

Who has the antonym for *valley*?

I have **maximum**.

Who has the antonym for *loose*?

I have **mountain**.

Who has the antonym for *help*?

I have **tight**.

Who has the antonym for *minor*?

I have **hurt**.

Who has the antonym for *drain*?

I have **major**.

Who has the antonym for *mend*?

I have **fill**.

Who has the antonym for *weird*?

I have **damage**.

Who has the antonym for *hide*?

I have **normal**.

Who has the first card?

Antonyms 3

Follow the path by highlighting the answers as your classmates identify them.

Where do snowmen keep their money?

START *	INCOMPLETE	HELPFUL	HURT	FILL
PERSEVERE	BELOW	REVEAL	MOUNTAIN	**FINISH** * NORMAL
VERTICAL	POLLUTE	DAMAGE	MAJOR	POLITE
CATCH	COWARDLY	THEY	TIGHT	KEEP
APPROXIMATE	SILLY	INCLUDE	MAXIMUM	IT
REPEL	COUNTERFEIT	CONTRACT	IN	SNOW
SOOTHE	BANKS	UGLY	STALE	TARDY
SADNESS	DEADLY	SUBTRACTION	SMOOTH	COUNTERCLOCKWISE
BLEND	EASY	INACTIVE	AVOID	DAWN
SHRINK	USEFUL	AGED	FREED	ORGANIZED

Start at the top left box of the chart and circle the first two words and the last two words that are **not** highlighted. Write the words that are **not** highlighted or circled in order below to solve the riddle.

__________ __________ __________ __________ __________ __________!

Write the words that are circled. Write an antonym for each word.

1. __________ = __________ 3. __________ = __________

2. __________ = __________ 4. __________ = __________

Antonyms 4

I have the **first card**.

Who has the antonym for *accept*?

I have **loan**.

Who has the antonym for *superior*?

I have **reject**.

Who has the antonym for *alive*?

I have **inferior**.

Who has the antonym for *tame*?

I have **deceased**.

Who has the antonym for *more*?

I have **wild**.

Who has the antonym for *wisdom*?

I have **less**.

Who has the antonym for *schedule*?

I have **foolishness**.

Who has the antonym for *probable*?

I have **cancel**.

Who has the antonym for *borrow*?

I have **improbable**.

Who has the antonym for *tried*?

Antonyms 4

I have **quit**.

Who has the antonym for *sharp*?

I have **land**.

Who has the antonym for *follow*?

I have **dull**.

Who has the antonym for *separate*?

I have **lead**.

Who has the antonym for *hold*?

I have **combine**.

Who has the antonym for *silly*?

I have **release**.

Who has the antonym for *legal*?

I have **serious**.

Who has the antonym for *fragrant*?

I have **illegal**.

Who has the antonym for *best*?

I have **stinky**.

Who has the antonym for *launch*?

I have **worst**.

Who has the antonym for *ruin*?

Antonyms 4

I have **improve**.

Who has the antonym for *mournful*?

I have **rival**.

Who has the antonym for *violent*?

I have **jolly**.

Who has the antonym for *even*?

I have **peaceful**.

Who has the antonym for *perfect*?

I have **odd**.

Who has the antonym for *relaxed*?

I have **defective**.

Who has the antonym for *know*?

I have **tense**.

Who has the antonym for *rising*?

I have **guess**.

Who has the antonym for *push*?

I have **falling**.

Who has the antonym for *partner*?

I have **pull**.

Who has the antonym for *freshen*?

Antonyms 4

I have **decay**.

Who has the antonym for *forget*?

I have **remove**.

Who has the antonym for *avoid*?

I have **remember**.

Who has the antonym for *rested*?

I have **face**.

Who has the antonym for *purchase*?

I have **exhausted**.

Who has the antonym for *deep*?

I have **sell**.

Who has the antonym for *encourage*?

I have **shallow**.

Who has the antonym for *hoard*?

I have **discourage**.

Who has the antonym for *sorrowful*?

I have **share**.

Who has the antonym for *replace*?

I have **funny**.

Who has the first card?

Antonyms 4

As your classmates identify the answers, highlight the letters that spell each antonym. Each new word is near the previous word. Words do not share letters and do not go backwards or diagonally. Clue: The first word is in the sixth column.

D	A	D	E	I	P	D	E	F	E	C	T	I	V	E	H	U	N	G	R	Y	O
I	F	I	X	D	U	G	O	S	O	F	T	P	E	A	C	E	F	U	L	F	I
F	U	S	H	E	L	U	L	O	O	B	U	S	Y	A	R	I	V	A	L	A	T
F	L	C	A	C	L	E	E	R	E	L	E	A	S	E	W	O	R	S	T	L	E
I	L	O	U	A	R	S	A	L	A	I	L	L	E	G	A	L	C	I	A	L	N
C	A	U	S	Y	E	S	D	A	E	R	O	T	T	E	N	A	O	M	J	I	S
U	F	R	T	R	J	E	A	N	E	S	E	R	I	O	U	S	M	P	O	N	E
L	U	A	E	E	E	E	O	D	S	T	I	N	K	Y	A	C	B	R	L	G	E
T	N	G	D	M	C	O	I	S	I	M	P	L	E	A	U	A	I	O	L	I	E
O	N	E	S	E	T	D	E	C	E	A	S	E	D	U	I	N	N	V	Y	I	A
R	Y	S	H	M	F	I	E	A	I	A	E	L	E	S	S	C	E	E	O	D	D
E	I	E	A	B	R	O	A	O	A	U	A	L	O	A	N	E	D	Q	O	A	R
M	F	L	L	E	E	A	W	I	N	F	E	R	I	O	R	L	U	U	I	F	O
O	A	L	L	R	S	U	I	I	O	A	E	I	O	U	A	E	L	I	U	L	U
V	C	O	O	A	H	O	L	E	A	U	N	E	V	E	N	E	L	T	O	A	G
E	E	I	W	E	A	I	D	A	I	M	P	R	O	B	A	B	L	E	I	T	H
S	H	A	R	E	F	O	O	L	I	S	H	N	E	S	S	I	I	D	L	E	O

Match the antonyms below and then find them in the areas of the word search you did **not** highlight.

1. _____ hungry
2. _____ flat
3. _____ busy
4. _____ soft
5. _____ fresh
6. _____ difficult

a. idle
b. rough
c. rotten
d. full
e. simple
f. uneven

HINT: If you did everything correctly, all the remaining letters are vowels.

Homophone Riddles

I have the **first card**.

Who has the two homophones that name an insect relative?

I have a **sweet suite**.

Who has the two homophones that describe some distasteful birds?

I have an **aunt ant**.

Who has the two homophones that name an animal with a sore throat?

I have **foul fowl**.

Who has the two homophones that mean run away insect?

I have a **hoarse horse**.

Who has the two homophones that mean a voting place flag stick?

I have **flee flea**.

Who has the two homophones that mean an uninterested plank of wood?

I have a **poll pole**.

Who has the two homophones that name a tired vegetable?

I have a **bored board**.

Who has the two homophones that mean a female forest mammal with money?

I have a **beat beet**.

Who has the two homophones that mean a sugary hotel room?

I have a **doe with dough**.

Who has the two homophones that mean an honest fee for travel?

Homophone Riddles

I have a **fair fare**.

Who has the two homophones that name what you did if you had a number for dinner?

I have **meet meat**.

Who has the two homophones that describe when an animal's feet stop?

I have **I ate eight**.

Who has the two homophones that mean a period of seven days that is not strong?

I have **paws pause**.

Who has the two homophones that mean a farewell purchase?

I have a **weak week**.

Who has the two homophones that mean a relative of a frog being pulled by something?

I have a **bye buy**.

Who has the two homophones that mean a penny odor?

I have a **towed toad**.

Who has the two homophones that mean an air transportation vehicle that is not fancy?

I have a **cent scent**.

Who has the two homophones that describe a complete opening?

I have a **plain plane**.

Who has the two homophones that show what happens when you introduce steak and pork?

I have a **whole hole**.

Who has the two homophones that name hair on a rabbit?

Homophone Riddles

I have **hare hair**.

Who has the two homophones that describe a hello on a mountaintop?

I have the **real reel**.

Who has the sound made by an inexpensive baby chick?

I have a **high hi**.

Who has the two homophones that name sixty minutes that belong to us?

I have a **cheap cheep**.

Who has the two homophones that mean tiny drops of water that you didn't feel?

I have **our hour**.

Who has the two homophones that mean money paid to the government for pointy metal objects?

I have a **missed mist**.

Who has the two homophones that mean a story about the wagging part of a dog?

I have **tacks tax**.

Who has the two homophones that name a type of tree along the edge of the ocean?

I have a **tail tale**.

Who has the two homophones that describe a grizzly forest mammal that has no clothes on?

I have a **beach beech**.

Who has the two homophones that name the genuine part of a fishing rod?

I have a **bare bear**.

Who has the two homophones that name the lines of thorny flowers in the garden?

Homophone Riddles

I have the **rose rows**.

Who has the two homophones that name what you call a female forest animal who is very important to you?

I have **I heard a herd**.

Who has the two homophones that name a squeaky sound made by a small stream?

I have a **dear deer**.

Who has the two homophones that name the only amount of money borrowed?

I have a **creek creak**.

Who has the two homophones that name the type of evening you see if a man is wearing a suit of armor?

I have the **lone loan**.

Who has the two homophones that name a boat trip the rowing teams took?

I have a **knight night**.

Who has the two homophones that name an area with very rough grass where people are playing golf?

I have the **crews' cruise**.

Who has the two homophones that name the glue put on the top of a room?

I have a **coarse course**.

Who has the two homophones that name mail received by a man?

I have the **ceiling sealing**.

Who has the two homophones that mean what you did if you listened to a group of cattle?

I have **male mail**.

Who has the first card?

Homophone Riddles

Follow the path by highlighting the answers as your classmates identify them.

LONE LOAN	CREWS' CRUISE	CEILING SEALING	I HEARD A HERD	CREEK CREAK	**FINISH** * MALE MAIL
DEAR DEER	ROSE ROWS	BARE BEAR	FLOWER FLOUR	KNIGHT NIGHT	COARSE COURSE
BLUE BLEW	KNEW NEW	TAIL TALE	EYE I	SEE SEA	WEIGHT WAIT
AUNT ANT	HOARSE HORSE	MISSED MIST	STEAL STEEL	HIGH HI	HARE HAIR
START *	POLL POLE	CHEAP CHEEP	MEAT MEET	OUR HOUR	WHOLE HOLE
SWEET SUITE	BEAT BEET	REAL REEL	BEACH BEECH	TACKS TAX	CENT SCENT
FOUL FOWL	FLEE FLEA	WAIST WASTE	MAID MADE	PALE PAIL	BYE BUY
DOE WITH DOUGH	BORED BOARD	WRITE RIGHT	RODE ROAD	MEET MEAT	PAWS PAUSE
FAIR FARE	I ATE EIGHT	WEAK WEEK	TOWED TOAD	PLAIN PLANE	SCENE SEEN

Look at the boxes that you did **not** highlight. Cross out the first box and every other one that is left over. Write the remaining pairs of homophones below.

__________ __________ __________ __________

__________ __________ __________ __________

__________ __________ __________ __________

__________ __________

Make up your own riddles for three pairs of homophones you wrote above. Write them on the back of this paper.

Homophone Spelling

Note: Explain to students that they will find the homophone for the underlined words.

I have the **first card**.

Who has the correct spelling of the homophone in this sentence:
A bear is an animal.

I have **w – a – s – t – e**.

Who has the correct spelling of the homophone in this sentence:
I got my hair cut.

I have **b – e – a – r**.

Who has the correct spelling of the homophone in this sentence:
It is dishonest to steal.

I have **h – a – i – r**.

Who has the correct spelling of the homophone in this sentence:
The rabbit was a male not a female.

I have **s – t – e – a – l**.

Who has the correct spelling of the homophone in this sentence:
Take me to the teacher!

I have **m – a – l – e**.

Who has the correct spelling of the homophone in this sentence:
My grandma likes to drink tea.

I have **t – o**.

Who has the correct spelling of the homophone in this sentence:
When it rains, it pours.

I have **t – e – a**.

Who has the correct spelling of the homophone in this sentence:
Please put your jacket over there.

I have **r – a – i – n – s**.

Who has the correct spelling of the homophone in this sentence:
You will waste it if you throw it away.

I have **t – h – e – r – e**.

Who has the correct spelling of the homophone in this sentence:
Would you like more sauce on your meat?

Homophone Spelling

Note: Explain to students that they will find the homophone for the underlined words.

I have **m – e – a – t**. Who has the correct spelling of the homophone in this sentence: Did you <u>write</u> the letter?	I have **p – a – i – l**. Who has the correct spelling of the homophone in this sentence: There's a <u>hole</u> in my pocket.
I have **w – r – i – t – e**. Who has the correct spelling of the homophone in this sentence: I'm feeling a bit <u>weak</u>.	I have **h – o – l – e**. Who has the correct spelling of the homophone in this sentence: He <u>knew</u> it wasn't his turn.
I have **w – e – a – k**. Who has the correct spelling of the homophone in this sentence: My shoelaces are tied in a <u>knot</u>.	I have **k – n – e – w**. Who has the correct spelling of the homophone in this sentence: Did you <u>hear</u> me calling you?
I have **k – n – o – t**. Who has the correct spelling of the homophone in this sentence: The wealthy woman had a <u>maid</u> to clean her house.	I have **h – e – a – r**. Who has the correct spelling of the homophone in this sentence: I'd like a <u>piece</u> of cake please.
I have **m – a – i – d**. Who has the correct spelling of the homophone in this sentence: Did you fill that <u>pail</u> with sand?	I have **p – i – e – c – e**. Who has the correct spelling of the homophone in this sentence: May I please have <u>two</u> scoops?

Homophone Spelling

Note: Explain to students that they will find the homophone for the underlined words.

I have **t – w – o**.

Who has the correct spelling of the homophone in this sentence:
I need you to sit <u>here</u>.

I have **r – e – i – n – s**.

Who has the correct spelling of the homophone in this sentence:
Was my answer <u>right</u>?

I have **h – e – r – e**.

Who has the correct spelling of the homophone in this sentence:
Has the <u>mail</u> been delivered yet?

I have **r – i – g – h – t**.

Who has the correct spelling of the homophone in this sentence:
I <u>made</u> that myself.

I have **m – a – i – l**.

Who has the correct spelling of the homophone in this sentence:
Where do you want to <u>meet</u> for dinner?

I have **m – a – d – e**.

Who has the correct spelling of the homophone in this sentence:
You ate a <u>whole</u> pizza?

I have **m – e – e – t**.

Who has the correct spelling of the homophone in this sentence:
Where is <u>their</u> house?

I have **w – h – o – l – e**.

Who has the correct spelling of the homophone in this sentence:
The soup is <u>too</u> hot.

I have **t – h – e – i – r**.

Who has the correct spelling of the homophone in this sentence:
Take the horse by the <u>reins</u>.

I have **t – o – o**.

Who has the correct spelling of the homophone in this sentence:
A <u>hare</u> moves by hopping.

Homophone Spelling

Note: Explain to students that they will find the homophone for the underlined words.

I have **h – a – r – e**.

Who has the correct spelling of the homophone in this sentence:
A belt goes around your <u>waist</u>.

I have **n – o – t**.

Who has the correct spelling of the homophone in this sentence:
The sick boy looks <u>pale.</u>

I have **w – a – i – s – t**.

Who has the correct spelling of the homophone in this sentence:
The house was made of <u>steel</u>.

I have **p – a – l – e**.

Who has the correct spelling of the homophone in this sentence:
I love your <u>new</u> shoes!

I have **s – t – e – e – l**.

Who has the correct spelling of the homophone in this sentence:
Did you walk in that puddle in your <u>bare</u> feet?

I have **n – e – w**.

Who has the correct spelling of the homophone in this sentence:
Mark placed the golf ball on a <u>tee</u>.

I have **b – a – r – e**.

Who has the correct spelling of the homophone in this sentence:
Is this your last <u>week</u>?

I have **t – e – e**.

Who has the correct spelling of the homophone in this sentence:
He spent every <u>cent</u> he had.

I have **w – e – e – k**.

Who has the correct spelling of the homophone in this sentence:
I will <u>not</u> tell you the answer.

I have **c – e – n – t**.

Who has the first card?

Homophone Spelling

As your classmates identify the answers, correctly write each homophone in the boxes below from left to right and top to bottom.

START →			
A	B	C	D

Write each word from Column D on the first set of lines. Write the homophone for the words on the second set of lines.
EXAMPLE: to = two

1. ______________ = ________________
2. ______________ = ________________
3. ______________ = ________________
4. ______________ = ________________
5. ______________ = ________________
6. ______________ = ________________
7. ______________ = ________________
8. ______________ = ________________
9. ______________ = ________________
10. ______________ = ________________

Compound Words

I have the **first card.**

Who has the rest of my compound word: rail____?

I have **lace.**

Who has the rest of my compound word: space ____?

I have **road.**

Who has the rest of my compound word: bed ____?

I have **ship.**

Who has the rest of my compound word: suit ____?

I have **spread.**

Who has the rest of my compound word: hand ____?

I have **case.**

Who has the rest of my compound word: door ____?

I have **shake.**

Who has the rest of my compound word: room ____?

I have **knob.**

Who has the rest of my compound word: wall ____?

I have **mate.**

Who has the rest of my compound word: shoe ____?

I have **paper.**

Who has the rest of my compound word: earth ____?

Compound Words

I have **quake**.

Who has the rest of my compound word: pop ____?

I have **meal**.

Who has the rest of my compound word: birth ____?

I have **corn**.

Who has the rest of my compound word: nut ____?

I have **day**.

Who has the rest of my compound word: clock ____?

I have **cracker**.

Who has the rest of my compound word: night ____?

I have **wise**.

Who has the rest of my compound word: country ____?

I have **gown**.

Who has the rest of my compound word: mail ____?

I have **side**.

Who has the rest of my compound word: chalk ____?

I have **box**.

Who has the rest of my compound word: oat ____?

I have **board**.

Who has the rest of my compound word: guide ____?

Compound Words

I have **book**.

Who has the rest of my compound word: fruit ____?

I have **sand**.

Who has the rest of my compound word: life ____?

I have **cake**.

Who has the rest of my compound word: flower ____?

I have **boat**.

Who has the rest of my compound word: horse ____?

I have **pot**.

Who has the rest of my compound word: mountain ____?

I have **back**.

Who has the rest of my compound word: lawn ____?

I have **top**.

Who has the rest of my compound word: master ____?

I have **mower**.

Who has the rest of my compound word: head ____?

I have **piece**.

Who has the rest of my compound word: quick ____?

I have **ache**.

Who has the rest of my compound word: thunder ____?

Compound Words

I have **storm**.

Who has the rest of my compound word: tooth ____?

I have **basket**.

Who has the rest of my compound word: water ____?

I have **paste**.

Who has the rest of my compound word: toad ____?

I have **color**.

Who has the rest of my compound word: scare ____?

I have **stool**.

Who has the rest of my compound word: lady ____?

I have **crow**.

Who has the rest of my compound word: rain ____?

I have **bug**.

Who has the rest of my compound word: touch ____?

I have **coat**.

Who has the rest of my compound word: sky ____?

I have **down**.

Who has the rest of my compound word: waste ____?

I have **scraper**.

Who has the first card?

Compound Words

As your classmates identify the answers, write the last part of each compound word in the boxes below from left to right and top to bottom.

START →			
A	**B**	**C**	**D**

In the box below are compound word beginnings. Combine each word beginning with a word ending from Column D to make compound words. EXAMPLE: rail + road = railroad

suit
oat
horse
milk
waste
pop
sky
cup
tooth
black

1. ____________ + ____________ = ____________

2. ____________ + ____________ = ____________

3. ____________ + ____________ = ____________

4. ____________ + ____________ = ____________

5. ____________ + ____________ = ____________

6. ____________ + ____________ = ____________

7. ____________ + ____________ = ____________

8. ____________ + ____________ = ____________

9. ____________ + ____________ = ____________

10. ____________ + ____________ = ____________

Compound Word Jokes

I have the **first card**.

Who has the answer to this joke:
Why is the bluebird blue?

I have **she wanted to catch starfish**.

Who has the answer to this joke:
Why did the girl put her cat on the photocopier?

I have **the mockingbird is always mocking him**.

Who has the answer to this joke:
Where do cars go when it gets hot?

I have **she wanted to have a copycat**.

Who has the answer to this joke:
Why did the boy put drumsticks in his ears?

I have **the carpool**.

Who has the answer to this joke:
Why did the man walk barefoot in the snow?

I have **he wanted to play his eardrums**.

Who has the answer to this joke:
Why did the man swallow the fire extinguisher?

I have **because his snowshoes melted**.

Who has the answer to this joke:
Why did the man take his goldfish to the bowling alley?

I have **he wanted to put out his heartburn**.

Who has the answer to this joke:
What dog keeps the best time?

I have **he wanted to see the fishbowl**.

Who has the answer to this joke:
Why did the lady take a fishing pole to the moon?

I have **a watchdog**.

Who has the answer to this joke:
Why did the twins feed grass to their frog?

Compound Word Jokes

I have **they wanted to have a grasshopper**.

Who has the answer to this joke: Why did the foolish girl drop her piece of bubble gum from the top of her roof?

I have **it was a blueberry**.

Who has the answer to this joke: What did the fruit lover pour all over his pancakes?

I have **she wanted to see a gumdrop**.

Who has the answer to this joke: What kind of nails do carpenters avoid?

I have **applesauce**.

Who has the answer to this joke: Why couldn't the girl get the crow out of her house?

I have **fingernails**.

Who has the answer to this joke: What horses swim the best?

I have **the crow thought it was in a birdhouse**.

Who has the answer to this joke: Why did the girl put her jewelry in her ear?

I have **seahorses**.

Who has the answer to this joke: Who is in charge of the library?

I have **she wanted to hear her earring**.

Who has the answer to this joke: Why did the boy walk instead of drive?

I have **the bookkeeper**.

Who has the answer to this joke: Why was the fruit so sad?

I have **he didn't want to get carsick**.

Who has the answer to this joke: Why did the farmer take his chickens to the beach?

Compound Word Jokes

I have **he wanted to get eggshells**.

Who has the answer to this joke: Why did the boy try to put his basketball in the television?

I have **a rainbow**.

Who has the answer to this joke: What time of the year is it when you are on a trampoline?

I have **he wanted a playstation**.

Who has the answer to this joke: What do you get if you cross a snowman with a vampire?

I have **springtime**.

Who has the answer to this joke: What do cows make during earthquakes?

I have **frostbite**.

Who has the answer to this joke: Where do snowmen keep their money?

I have **milkshakes**.

Who has the answer to this joke: What washes up on very small beaches?

I have **in snowbanks**.

Who has the answer to this joke: What did the spider make on the computer?

I have **microwaves**.

Who has the answer to this joke: What do lawyers wear to court?

I have **a website**.

Who has the answer to this joke: What bow can't be tied?

I have **lawsuits**.

Who has the answer to this joke: What kind of button won't unbutton?

Compound Word Jokes

I have **a bellybutton**.

Who has the answer to this joke: What does a shark eat with peanut butter?

I have **a groundhog**.

Who has the answer to this joke: What dance will a chicken not do?

I have **jellyfish**.

Who has the answer to this joke: When do you stop at green and go at red?

I have **the foxtrot**.

Who has the answer to this joke: What do you call a sleeping bull?

I have **when you eat a watermelon**.

Who has the answer to this joke: Why don't the mountains get cold in the winter?

I have **a bulldozer**.

Who has the answer to this joke: What do you get when a chicken lays an egg on top of a slide?

I have **because they wear snowcaps**.

Who has the answer to this joke: What do you get if you cross a steer with a tadpole?

I have **an eggroll**.

Who has the answer to this joke: What do you call a hungry ant?

I have **a bullfrog**.

Who has the answer to this joke: What do you get if you cross a pile of mud with a pig?

I have **an anteater**.

Who has the first card?

Compound Word Jokes

Follow the path by highlighting the answers as your classmates identify them.

START *	THE MOCKINGBIRD IS ALWAYS MOCKING HIM	THE CARPOOL	CATFISH
A WATCHDOG	HE WANTED TO PUT OUT HIS HEARTBURN	BECAUSE HIS SNOWSHOES MELTED	HE WANTED TO SEE THE FISHBOWL
THEY WANTED TO HAVE A GRASSHOPPER	HE WANTED TO PLAY HIS EARDRUMS	SHE WANTED TO HAVE A COPYCAT	SHE WANTED TO CATCH STARFISH
SHE WANTED TO SEE A GUMDROP	FINGERNAILS	HORSESHOE	RAILROAD
THE BOOKKEEPER	SEAHORSES	AN EGGROLL	**FINISH** * AN ANTEATER
IT WAS A BLUEBERRY	POPCORN	A BULLDOZER	ROADMAP
APPLESAUCE	SHOELACE	THE FOXTROT	REDBIRD
THE CROW THOUGHT IT WAS IN A BIRDHOUSE	CARHOP	A GROUNDHOG	BACKYARD
SHE WANTED TO HEAR HER EARRING	BLACKBERRY	A BULLFROG	SPACESHIP
HE DIDN'T WANT TO GET CARSICK	HOUSEFLY	BECAUSE THEY WEAR SNOWCAPS	WHEN YOU EAT A WATERMELON
HE WANTED TO GET EGGSHELLS	HE WANTED A PLAYSTATION	TEACUP	JELLYFISH
IN SNOWBANKS	FROSTBITE	HEADLIGHT	A BELLYBUTTON
A WEBSITE	MILKSHAKES	MICROWAVES	LAWSUITS
A RAINBOW	SPRINGTIME	SUNLIGHT	COUNTRYSIDE

Choose three compound words that you did **not** highlight. Then write sentences using each compound word.

1. ______________________________

2. ______________________________

3. ______________________________

Making Compound Words

I have the **first card**.

Who has the word that can go in front of *flower*, *light*, and *day* to make three compound words?

I have **blue**.

Who has the word that can go in front of *town, run,* and *made* to make three compound words?

I have **sun**.

Who has the word that can go in front of *port, plane,* and *line* to make three compound words?

I have **home**.

Who has the word that can go in front of *band, ache,* and *quarters* to make three compound words?

I have **air**.

Who has the word that can go in front of *thing, what,* and *times* to make three compound words?

I have **head**.

Who has the word that can go in front of *hold, fly,* and *keeper* to make three compound words?

I have **some**.

Who has the word that can go in front of *lids, glasses*, and *balls* to make three compound words?

I have **house**.

Who has the word that can go in front of *side, weed,* and *shore* to make three compound words?

I have **eye**.

Who has the word that can go in front of *jay, fish,* and *berry* to make three compound words?

I have **sea**.

Who has the word that can go in front of *stone, box,* and *paper* to make three compound words?

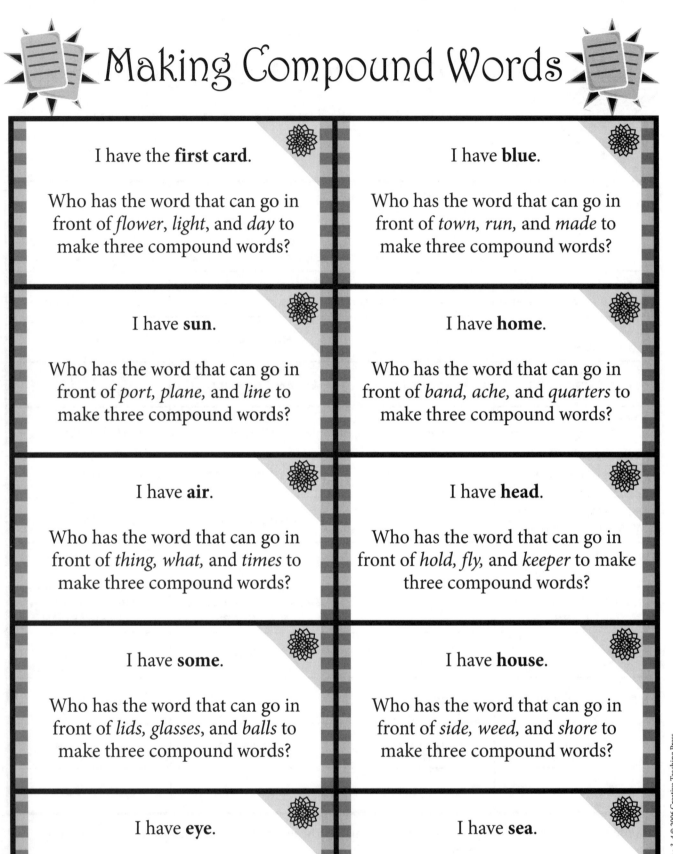

Making Compound Words

I have **sand**.

Who has the word that can go in front of *moon, bee,* and *dew* to make three compound words?

I have **some**.

Who has the word that can go in front of *place, time,* and *way* to make three compound words?

I have **honey**.

Who has the word that can go in front of *pick, ache,* and *paste* to make three compound words?

I have **any**.

Who has the word that can go in front of *hand, stage,* and *pack* to make three compound words?

I have **tooth**.

Who has the word that can go in front of *bow, check,* and *coat* to make three compound words?

I have **back**.

Who has the word that can go in front of *water, wear,* and *age* to make three compound words?

I have **rain**.

Who has the word that can go in front of *power, natural,* and *market* to make three compound words?

I have **under**.

Who has the word that can go in front of *shelf, store,* and *worm* to make three compound words?

I have **super**.

Who has the word that can go in front of *body, day,* and *how* to make three compound words?

I have **book**.

Who has the word that can go in front of *guard, boat,* and *long* to make three compound words?

Making Compound Words

I have **life**.

Who has the word that can go in front of *head, finger,* and *father* to make three compound words?

I have **car**.

Who has the word that can go in front of *father, parent,* and *child* to make three compound words?

I have **fore**.

Who has the word that can go in front of *print, nail,* and *tack* to make three compound words?

I have **grand**.

Who has the word that can go in front of *line, show,* and *step* to make three compound words?

I have **thumb**.

Who has the word that can go in front of *out, bird,* and *berries* to make three compound words?

I have **side**.

Who has the word that can go in front of *stand, print,* and *paper* to make three compound words?

I have **black**.

Who has the word that can go in front of *time, break,* and *dream* to make three compound words?

I have **news**.

Who has the word that can go in front of *cap, bank,* and *drift* to make three compound words?

I have **day**.

Who has the word that can go in front of *sick, go,* and *pet* to make three compound words?

I have **snow**.

Who has the word that can go in front of *saver, keeper,* and *clock* to make three compound words?

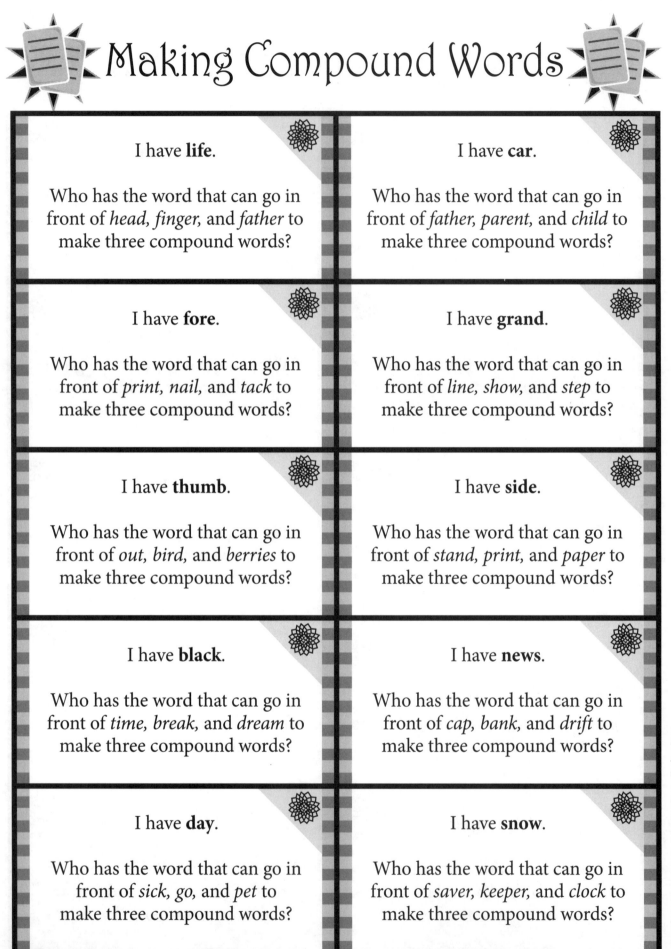

Making Compound Words

I have **time**.

Who has the word that can go in front of *top, spoon,* and *cloth* to make three compound words?

I have **flower**.

Who has the word that can go in front of *side, door,* and *numbered* to make three compound words?

I have **table**.

Who has the word that can go in front of *cake, bread,* and *stop* to make three compound words?

I have **out**.

Who has the word that can go in front of *apple, cone,* and *nut* to make three compound words?

I have **short**.

Who has the word that can go in front of *pen, tail,* and *skin* to make three compound words?

I have **pine**.

Who has the word that can go in front of *horse, track,* and *car* to make three compound words?

I have **pig**.

Who has the word that can go in front of *hose, fighter,* and *wood* to make three compound words?

I have **race**.

Who has the word that can go in front of *time, kettle,* and *spoon* to make three compound words?

I have **fire**.

Who has the word that can go in front of *pot, bud,* and *petal* to make three compound words?

I have **tea**.

Who has the first card?

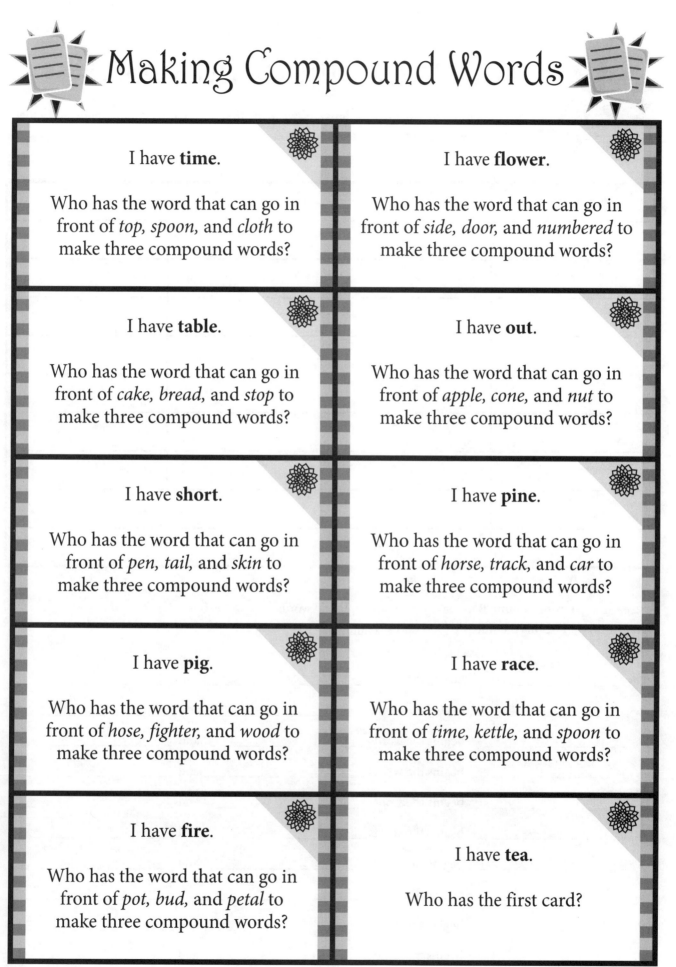

Making Compound Words

As your classmates identify the answers, write the first part of each compound word in the boxes below from left to right and top to bottom.

START →			
A	B	C	D

Use each word from Column B to make two new compound words.
EXAMPLE: <u>air</u> begins the words <u>airport</u> and <u>airplane</u>

1. ____________ begins the words ____________ and ____________
2. ____________ begins the words ____________ and ____________
3. ____________ begins the words ____________ and ____________
4. ____________ begins the words ____________ and ____________
5. ____________ begins the words ____________ and ____________
6. ____________ begins the words ____________ and ____________
7. ____________ begins the words ____________ and ____________
8. ____________ begins the words ____________ and ____________
9. ____________ begins the words ____________ and ____________
10. ____________ begins the words ____________ and ____________

Nouns

I have the **first card**.

Who has the noun in this sentence:
Where is my new jacket?

I have **movie**.

Who has the noun in this sentence:
The busy carpenter earned $50.00.

I have **jacket**.

Who has the noun in this sentence:
That bee almost stung me!

I have **carpenter**.

Who has the noun in this sentence:
I need to drink more water.

I have **bee**.

Who has the noun in this sentence:
When does school start?

I have **water**.

Who has the noun in this sentence:
When does that huge plane leave?

I have **school**.

Who has the noun in this sentence:
May I please have some more strawberries?

I have **plane**.

Who has the noun in this sentence:
She watched the red balloon float away.

I have **strawberries**.

Who has the noun in this sentence:
The scary movie was so fun to watch!

I have **balloon**.

Who has the noun in this sentence:
He raised his hand quickly.

Nouns

I have **hand**.

Who has the noun in this sentence: This chocolate chip cookie is delicious.

I have **calendar**.

Who has the noun in this sentence: She tripped over her own shoe.

I have **cookie**.

Who has the noun in this sentence: Where is your baseball glove?

I have **shoe**.

Who has the noun in this sentence: That painting is crooked.

I have **glove**.

Who has the noun in this sentence: Who will take out the trash?

I have **painting**.

Who has the noun in this sentence: It was so dark in the cave I nearly screamed!

I have **trash**.

Who has the noun in this sentence: I can't find my history book.

I have **cave**.

Who has the noun in this sentence: Do you have enough money to buy it?

I have **book**.

Who has the noun in this sentence: I bought a new calendar.

I have **money**.

Who has the noun in this sentence: The tired farmer decided to rest.

Nouns

I have **farmer**.

Who has the noun in this sentence:
Look at the mallard ducks
flying up there.

I have **carrots**.

Who has the noun in this sentence:
The ancient tower is leaning.

I have **ducks**.

Who has the noun in this sentence:
My new puppy is soft and cuddly.

I have **tower**.

Who has the noun in this sentence:
The mystery novel is thrilling to read.

I have **puppy**.

Who has the noun in this sentence:
I love your new blue carpet.

I have **novel**.

Who has the noun in this sentence:
I see a red truck.

I have **carpet**.

Who has the noun in this sentence:
The fabric is torn.

I have **truck**.

Who has the noun in this sentence:
The circus clowns were funny.

I have **fabric**.

Who has the noun in this sentence:
Those fresh carrots are for me.

I have **clowns**.

Who has the noun in this sentence:
He dove into the deep pool.

Nouns

I have **pool**.

Who has the noun in this sentence:
The radio was broken.

I have **dream**.

Who has the noun in this sentence:
The vacant house is ready to be sold.

I have **radio**.

Who has the noun in this sentence:
That cereal is too sugary for you to eat.

I have **house**.

Who has the noun in this sentence:
Where is the new campground located?

I have **cereal**.

Who has the noun in this sentence:
The mouse ran quickly.

I have **campground**.

Who has the noun in this sentence:
What a terrific treehouse!

I have **mouse**.

Who has the noun in this sentence:
The sports car sped away.

I have **treehouse**.

Who has the noun in this sentence:
Her country report was very good.

I have **car**.

Who has the noun in this sentence:
My dream was scary.

I have **report**.

Who has the first card?

Nouns

As your classmates identify the answers, highlight the letters that spell each noun. Each new word is near the previous word. Words do not share letters and do not go backwards or diagonally. Clue: The first word is in the last column.

C	A	M	P	G	R	O	U	N	D	H	N	O	U	S	I	G	N
T	N	T	C	L	O	W	N	S	P	O	M	O	T	O	R	C	M
R	O	R	N	B	N	C	O	C	O	U	S	T	O	V	E	A	O
E	V	U	U	O	N	A	F	A	O	S	D	R	E	A	M	R	U
E	E	C	N	O	O	R	A	R	L	E	C	E	R	E	A	L	S
H	L	K	U	K	N	R	B	P	R	A	D	I	O	D	N	T	E
O	T	O	W	E	R	O	R	E	O	U	N	N	O	U	U	O	N
U	N	O	U	C	N	T	I	T	P	U	P	P	Y	C	S	W	J
S	N	T	O	A	U	S	C	F	A	R	M	E	R	K	C	E	A
E	R	E	N	V	M	O	N	E	Y	N	O	U	S	S	H	R	C
W	E	L	N	E	P	A	I	N	T	I	N	G	H	N	O	B	K
A	P	E	T	O	C	A	L	E	N	D	A	R	O	U	O	E	E
T	O	V	R	B	O	O	K	N	N	O	U	N	E	N	L	E	T
C	R	I	A	O	M	S	T	R	A	W	B	E	R	R	I	E	S
H	T	S	S	G	O	C	A	R	P	E	N	T	E	R	W	P	T
B	U	I	H	L	V	N	H	N	O	P	L	A	N	E	A	A	R
A	U	O	N	O	I	N	A	B	A	L	L	O	O	N	T	P	E
N	O	N	U	V	E	N	N	A	N	I	M	A	L	N	E	E	E
D	O	U	N	E	N	O	D	R	A	B	B	I	T	U	R	R	N
N	O	U	C	O	O	K	I	E	N	B	A	S	E	B	A	L	L

The following nouns are also hidden in the word search. Locate each word and then use it in a complete sentence. Write your sentences on the back of this paper.

1. baseball
2. television
3. watchband
4. sign
5. rabbit
6. tree
7. stove
8. animal
9. motor
10. paper
11. tower
12. book

HINT: If you did everything correctly, the remaining letters will spell the word *noun* many times.

Adjectives

I have the **first card**.

Who has the adjective in this sentence: Is that your tiny dollhouse?

I have **broken**.

Who has the adjective in this sentence: The little girl loved her party.

I have **tiny**.

Who has the adjective in this sentence: She loves her curly hair.

I have **little**.

Who has the adjective in this sentence: The cuddly bunny is sleeping.

I have **curly**.

Who has the adjective in this sentence: The bridge was too narrow to cross.

I have **cuddly**.

Who has the adjective in this sentence: The train was slow.

I have **narrow**.

Who has the adjective in this sentence: The classroom was silent.

I have **slow**.

Who has the adjective in this sentence: He waited in the noisy subway.

I have **silent**.

Who has the adjective in this sentence: The broken glass was thrown away.

I have **noisy**.

Who has the adjective in this sentence: There were few cookies left.

Adjectives

I have **few**.

Who has the adjective in this sentence: She has many books in her library.

I have **fluffy**.

Who has the adjective in this sentence: He ate the juicy apple.

I have **many**.

Who has the adjective in this sentence: The damaged road was repaired.

I have **juicy**.

Who has the adjective in this sentence: The nervous girl cried.

I have **damaged**.

Who has the adjective in this sentence: The dry air made me sneeze.

I have **nervous**.

Who has the adjective in this sentence: A sticky lollipop is stuck to the shoe.

I have **dry**.

Who has the adjective in this sentence: The petite girl shopped for a dress.

I have **sticky**.

Who has the adjective in this sentence: What a mysterious letter he received!

I have **petite**.

Who has the adjective in this sentence: Her fluffy blanket is on the bed.

I have **mysterious**.

Who has the adjective in this sentence: The funny girl was telling jokes.

Adjectives

I have **funny**.

Who has the adjective in this sentence: Did you eat that stale bread?

I have **screeching**.

Who has the adjective in this sentence: Did you see that foolish man?

I have **stale**.

Who has the adjective in this sentence: What happened to the wicked witch?

I have **foolish**.

Who has the adjective in this sentence: Is that the courageous boy who saved the puppy?

I have **wicked**.

Who has the adjective in this sentence: She saw the massive castle on her tour.

I have **courageous**.

Who has the adjective in this sentence: Who made that tasty spaghetti?

I have **massive**.

Who has the adjective in this sentence: The empty box was recycled.

I have **tasty**.

Who has the adjective in this sentence: I spread melted butter on the potato.

I have **empty**.

Who has the adjective in this sentence: The sound of screeching tires scared the baby.

I have **melted**.

Who has the adjective in this sentence: The angry wasp stung the boy.

Adjectives

I have **angry**.

Who has the adjective in this sentence: The crooked line was hard to trace.

I have **loose**.

Who has the adjective in this sentence: There was a strong odor coming from the trashcan.

I have **crooked**.

Who has the adjective in this sentence: Have you been inside that creepy house?

I have **strong**.

Who has the adjective in this sentence: The hungry cat ate the food.

I have **creepy**.

Who has the adjective in this sentence: The late bus finally arrived.

I have **hungry**.

Who has the adjective in this sentence: The confused student wisely asked for help.

I have **late**.

Who has the adjective in this sentence: The spicy sauce burned her mouth.

I have **confused**.

Who has the adjective in this sentence: I dropped the greasy bacon on the floor.

I have **spicy**.

Who has the adjective in this sentence: Have you seen my loose tooth?

I have **greasy**.

Who has the first card?

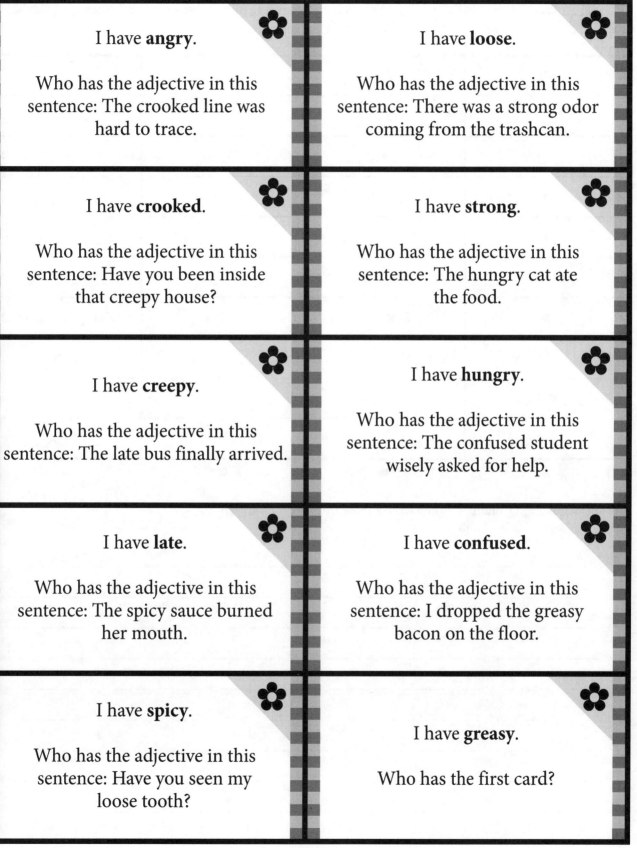

Adjectives

Fill in the missing letters of the adjectives as your classmates identify them. Start at the arrow and go from left to right and top to bottom.

A	B	C	D
→	_ I _ _	_ U _ _ _	_ A _ _ _ W
_ I _ _ _ _	_ _ O _ E _	_ _ _ _ _ E	_ U _ _ _ Y
_ _ _ W	_ _ I _ _	_ _ W	_ _ _ Y
_ A _ A _ _ D	_ _ Y	_ _ _ I _ _	_ _ U _ _ _
_ _ I _ _	_ _ _ _ O U _	_ _ _ _ _ Y	_ Y _ _ _ _ I O U _
_ U _ _ _	_ _ _ _ E	_ _ _ _ E _	_ A _ _ I _ _
_ _ P _ _	_ _ _ E E _ _ _ _ _ _	_ _ _ _ I _ _	_ O U _ A _ E O U _
_ _ _ _ Y	_ E _ _ _ _	_ _ _ _ Y	_ _ O O _ _ _
_ _ E E _ _	_ _ _ E	_ _ I _ _	_ _ _ _ E
_ _ _ O _ _	_ U _ _ _ Y	_ O _ _ _ _ _ _ _	_ _ E A _ _

List the words from Column C. Then write a sentence using each adjective.

1. ________ ________________________
2. ________ ________________________
3. ________ ________________________
4. ________ ________________________
5. ________ ________________________
6. ________ ________________________
7. ________ ________________________
8. ________ ________________________
9. ________ ________________________
10. ________ ________________________

Verbs

I have the **first card**.

Who has the verb in this sentence:
Let's climb that tree over there.

I have **climb**.

Who has the verb in this sentence:
May I buy a milkshake?

I have **buy**.

Who has the verb in this sentence:
Dad drives me to school.

I have **drives**.

Who has the verb in this sentence:
When did the glass break?

I have **break**.

Who has the verb in this sentence:
The airplane landed at Gate 4b.

I have **landed**.

Who has the verb in this sentence:
Rob designed that robot all
by himself.

I have **designed**.

Who has the verb in this sentence:
The water freezes to make ice.

I have **freezes**.

Who has the verb in this sentence:
Carlos escaped.

I have **escaped**.

Who has the verb in this sentence:
My magazine subscription
expires next month.

I have **expires**.

Who has the verb in this sentence:
She should recover from the flu
in a few days.

Verbs

I have **recover**.

Who has the verb in this sentence:
The penguins waddled to the water.

I have **rode**.

Who has the verb in this sentence:
I come to school prepared.

I have **waddled**.

Who has the verb in this sentence:
Please raise your hand.

I have **come**.

Who has the verb in this sentence:
Maria hung on the bars for one minute.

I have **raise**.

Who has the verb in this sentence:
The boys wandered through the forest.

I have **hung**.

Who has the verb in this sentence:
The museum purchased the original picture.

I have **wandered**.

Who has the verb in this sentence:
The quarterback passed the ball.

I have **purchased**.

Who has the verb in this sentence:
The vines are creeping up the wall.

I have **passed**.

Who has the verb in this sentence:
Omar rode the horse.

I have **are creeping**.

Who has the verb in this sentence:
He will retire in June.

Verbs

I have **will retire**.

Who has the verb in this sentence: Peter invented an interesting contraption.

I have **examined**.

Who has the verb in this sentence: Now retell the story from the very beginning.

I have **invented**.

Who has the verb in this sentence: Let's compare the frogs with the toads.

I have **retell**.

Who has the verb in this sentence: She adopted her new dog from a shelter.

I have **compare**.

Who has the verb in this sentence: Please translate this letter for me.

I have **adopted**.

Who has the verb in this sentence: He listed the groceries in alphabetical order.

I have **translate**.

Who has the verb in this sentence: I choose my own clothes in the morning.

I have **listed**.

Who has the verb in this sentence: She built the model airplane all by herself.

I have **choose**.

Who has the verb in this sentence: The doctor examined the sick patient.

I have **built**.

Who has the verb in this sentence: They debated the topics for hours.

Verbs

I have **debated**.

Who has the verb in this sentence:
The man owns several businesses.

I have **will discuss**.

Who has the verb in this sentence:
Next, draw a diagram of the information.

I have **owns**.

Who has the verb in this sentence:
The company employs 2,000 workers.

I have **draw**.

Who has the verb in this sentence:
Now you can trace the picture carefully.

I have **employs**.

Who has the verb in this sentence:
She interviewed for the job last week.

I have **can trace**.

Who has the verb in this sentence:
You deserve a reward.

I have **interviewed**.

Who has the verb in this sentence:
Please compute the total cost for me.

I have **deserve**.

Who has the verb in this sentence:
He estimated the number of marbles in the jar.

I have **compute**.

Who has the verb in this sentence:
I will discuss the topics for your reports.

I have **estimated**.

Who has the first card?

Verbs

Follow the path by highlighting the answers as your classmates identify them.

CLIMB	**START** *	ATE	DRINK	WATCH	CLIMB
BUY	READ	DEBATED	OWNS	EMPLOYS	**FINISH** * ESTIMATED
DRIVES	BREAK	BUILT	DESCRIBE	INTERVIEWED	DESERVE
DESIGNED	LANDED	LISTED	ADOPTED	COMPUTE	CAN TRACE
FREEZES	COOK	WRITE	RETELL	WILL DISCUSS	DRAW
ESCAPED	EXPIRES	SAY	EXAMINED	COMPARE	INVENTED
EXPLAIN	RECOVER	PLANTING	CHOOSE	TRANSLATE	WILL RETIRE
RAISE	WADDLED	ASSISTED	DROVE	HELPING	ARE CREEPING
WANDERED	PASSED	RODE	COME	HUNG	PURCHASED

Cross out the first word that is **not** highlighted and every other word. Write the verbs that are **not** highlighted or crossed out. Use each verb in a sentence.

1. ______________ ____

2. ______________ ____

3. ______________ ____

4. ______________ ____

5. ______________ ____

6. ______________ ____

7. ______________ ____

Adverbs

I have the **first card**.

Who has the adverb in this sentence: He kindly shared his last chocolate brownie.

I have **neatly**.

Who has the adverb in this sentence: He suddenly fell off his new skateboard.

I have **kindly**.

Who has the adverb in this sentence: They read their books quietly in the warm tent.

I have **suddenly**.

Who has the adverb in this sentence: The dog lazily napped on the bed.

I have **quietly**.

Who has the adverb in this sentence: She truthfully told of how she lost her homework.

I have **lazily**.

Who has the adverb in this sentence: Did you accidentally drop that expensive vase?

I have **truthfully**.

Who has the adverb in this sentence: The child foolishly put the dirty spoon in her mouth.

I have **accidentally**.

Who has the adverb in this sentence: She solved puzzles daily to keep her mind strong.

I have **foolishly**.

Who has the adverb in this sentence: The blue sheets were neatly put away.

I have **daily**.

Who has the adverb in this sentence: Did you see how he selfishly used the last stamp?

Adverbs

I have **selfishly**.

Who has the adverb in this sentence:
She warmly thanked her friend
for the unexpected gift.

I have **far**.

Who has the adverb in this sentence:
Can you believe that I rarely
watch television?

I have **warmly**.

Who has the adverb in this sentence:
They arrived safely home from
their trip.

I have **rarely**.

Who has the adverb in this sentence:
The coach spoke loudly so the
players could hear him.

I have **safely**.

Who has the adverb in this sentence:
She was feeling really sick on her
family vacation.

I have **loudly**.

Who has the adverb in this sentence:
The snail crossed the path cautiously.

I have **really**.

Who has the adverb in this sentence:
He was nervously tapping his
fingers on the table.

I have **cautiously**.

Who has the adverb in this sentence:
He correctly answered the
difficult question.

I have **nervously**.

Who has the adverb in this sentence:
They drove far across the
spacious countryside.

I have **correctly**.

Who has the adverb in this sentence:
She calmly listened to his argument.

Adverbs

I have **calmly**.

Who has the adverb in this sentence: Her dress flowed elegantly across the dance floor.

I have **often**.

Who has the adverb in this sentence: They politely said they were not hungry.

I have **elegantly**.

Who has the adverb in this sentence: He cheerfully accepted his new job.

I have **politely**.

Who has the adverb in this sentence: She brushed her dog's hair gently.

I have **cheerfully**.

Who has the adverb in this sentence: Did you notice how thoughtfully she wrote that letter?

I have **gently**.

Who has the adverb in this sentence: It's amazing how the twins seldom argue.

I have **thoughtfully**.

Who has the adverb in this sentence: He ate less for breakfast yesterday.

I have **seldom**.

Who has the adverb in this sentence: The code was successfully broken.

I have **less**.

Who has the adverb in this sentence: Do you thank your family often?

I have **successfully**.

Who has the adverb in this sentence: They opened the door carefully.

Adverbs

I have **carefully**.

Who has the adverb in this sentence: They played on the slide briefly during recess.

I have **violently**.

Who has the adverb in this sentence: He almost won first prize.

I have **briefly**.

Who has the adverb in this sentence: They arrived at school promptly on their first day.

I have **almost**.

Who has the adverb in this sentence: Mrs. Smith fairly gave each student the same number of stickers.

I have **promptly**.

Who has the adverb in this sentence: They followed the rules obediently at school.

I have **fairly**.

Who has the adverb in this sentence: Did you see how gracefully the ballerinas moved?

I have **obediently**.

Who has the adverb in this sentence: Can you believe that they rudely asked for more pudding?

I have **gracefully**.

Who has the adverb in this sentence: They sadly admitted what they had done.

I have **rudely**.

Who has the adverb in this sentence: The waves crashed violently on the shore.

I have **sadly**.

Who has the first card?

Adverbs

Fill in the missing letters of the adverbs as your classmates identify them. Start at the arrow and go from left to right and top to bottom.

→	_ I _ _ _ _	_ _ _ E _ _ _	_ _ U _ _ _ U _ _ _
_ _ _ _ I _ _ _ _	_ E _ _ _ _	_ U _ _ E _ _ _	_ _ _ I _ _
A _ _ I _ E _ _ A _ _ Y	_ A _ _ _	_ E _ _ _ _ _ _ _	_ A _ _ _ _
_ _ _ E _ _	_ _ A _ _ _	_ E _ _ O U _ _ _	_ A _
_ _ _ E _ _	_ _ U _ _ _	_ A U _ I O U _ _ _	_ O _ _ _ C _ _ _
_ A _ _ _ _	E _ E _ _ _ _ _ _	_ _ E _ _ _ _ _ _ _	_ _ O U _ _ _ _ _ _ _
_ E _ _	O _ T _ _	_ _ _ I _ E _ _	_ E _ _ _ _
_ E _ _ _ _	_ U _ _ E _ _ _ _ _ _	_ A _ E _ _ _ _ _	_ _ I E _ _ _
_ _ O _ P T _ _	_ _ E _ I E _ _ _ _	_ _ _ E _ _	_ _ _ _ E _ _ _ _
A _ _ _ _ _	_ A I _ _ _	_ _ _ _ E _ _ _ _ _	_ A _ _ _
A	**B**	**C**	**D**

Write the adverbs from Column B. Then write a sentence using each adverb.

1. ______________ ____
2. ______________ ____
3. ______________ ____
4. ______________ ____
5. ______________ ____
6. ______________ ____
7. ______________ ____
8. ______________ ____
9. ______________ ____
10. ______________ ____

Collective Nouns

I have the **first card**.

Who has a group of ants?

I have a **flock**.

Who has a group of buffalo?

I have an **army**.

Who has a group of baboons?

I have a **herd**.

Who has a group of cats?

I have a **tribe**.

Who has a group of beavers?

I have a **litter**.

Who has a group of dogs?

I have a **colony**.

Who has a group of bees?

I have a **pack**.

Who has a group of fish?

I have a **swarm**.

Who has a group of birds?

I have a **school**.

Who has a group of geese?

Collective Nouns

I have a **gaggle**.

Who has a group of gnats?

I have a **belt**.

Who has a group of ships?

I have a **horde**.

Who has a group of horses?

I have a **fleet**.

Who has a group of mountains?

I have a **team**.

Who has a group of clams?

I have a **range**.

Who has a group of lions?

I have a **bed**.

Who has a group of actors?

I have a **pride**.

Who has a group of whales?

I have a **cast**.

Who has a group of asteroids?

I have a **pod**.

Who has a group of soldiers?

Collective Nouns

I have a **platoon**.

Who has a group of employees?

I have a **crowd**.

Who has a group of stairs?

I have a **staff**.

Who has a group of islands?

I have a **flight**.

Who has a group of books?

I have a **chain**.

Who has a group of students?

I have a **library**.

Who has a group of computers?

I have a **class**.

Who has a group of athletes?

I have a **network**.

Who has a group of cards?

I have a **team**.

Who has a group of onlookers?

I have a **deck**.

Who has a group of bread loaves?

Collective Nouns

I have a **batch**.

Who has a group of camels?

I have a **quiver**.

Who has a group of keys?

I have a **caravan**.

Who has a group of jewels?

I have a **ring**.

Who has a group of penguins?

I have a **cache**.

Who has a group of sailors?

I have a **rookery**.

Who has a group of experts?

I have a **crew**.

Who has a group of hand-picked flowers?

I have a **panel**.

Who has a group of tasks?

I have a **bouquet**.

Who has a group of arrows?

I have a **list**.

Who has the first card?

Collective Nouns

Follow the path by highlighting the answers as your classmates identify them.

TEAM	BED	CLUSTER	RANGE	PRIDE	POD
HORDE	CAST	BELT	FLEET	STREAK	PLATOON
GAGGLE	SCHOOL	STRING	TROUPE	CHAIN	STAFF
BUNCH	PACK	BROOD	ATLAS	CLASS	TEAM
HERD	LITTER	BOUQUET	CREW	BAND	CROWD
FLOCK	SWARM	QUIVER	CACHE	CARAVAN	FLIGHT
ARMY	COLONY	RING	PANEL	BATCH	LIBRARY
START *	TRIBE	ROOKERY	LIST FINISH*	DECK	NETWORK

Write each word you did **not** highlight. Write what the collective noun identifies as a group.

1.____________________ is a collective noun that identifies a group of ____________________

2.____________________ is a collective noun that identifies a group of ____________________

3.____________________ is a collective noun that identifies a group of ____________________

4.____________________ is a collective noun that identifies a group of ____________________

5.____________________ is a collective noun that identifies a group of ____________________

6.____________________ is a collective noun that identifies a group of ____________________

7.____________________ is a collective noun that identifies a group of ____________________

8.____________________ is a collective noun that identifies a group of ____________________

Tenses—Past, Present, or Future?

I have the **first card**.

Who has a sentence about a baby with a past tense verb?

I have the sentence
The baby cried.

Who has a sentence about soccer with a present tense verb?

I have the sentence
They are playing soccer at the park.

Who has a sentence about a vacation with a future tense verb?

I have the sentence
I will be leaving for my vacation next week.

Who has a sentence about socks with a past tense verb?

I have the sentence
I lost my socks last week at camp.

Who has a sentence about cookies with a present tense verb?

I have the sentence
Are the cookies burning?

Who has a sentence about a table with a past tense verb?

I have the sentence
The leg of the table broke during dinner.

Who has a sentence about fruit with a future tense verb?

I have the sentence
The oranges will be ripe in two weeks.

Who has a sentence about a lake with a present tense verb?

I have the sentence
The waves on the lake are so smooth.

Who has a sentence about rabbits with a past tense verb?

I have the sentence
It all started three months ago with two rabbits.

Who has a sentence about camping with a future tense verb?

I Have, Who Has?: Language Arts • 3–4 © 2006 Creative Teaching Press

Tenses—Past, Present, or Future?

I have the sentence
They will be coming home from the camping trip.

Who has a sentence about a picnic with a present tense verb?

I have the sentence
Will your baby be a boy or a girl?

Who has a sentence about fruit with a past tense verb?

I have the sentence
Why are there so many ants here?

Who has a sentence about a turtle with a past tense verb?

I have the sentence
The apples were picked last week.

Who has a sentence about rabbits with a present tense verb?

I have the sentence
The turtle won the race.

Who has a sentence about a broken arm with a future tense verb?

I have the sentence
We have seven pet rabbits.

Who has a sentence about a broken arm with a past tense verb?

I have the sentence
You will break your arm if you climb that mountain!

Who has a sentence about a vacation with a present tense verb?

I have the sentence
He broke his arm when he fell off the mountain.

Who has a sentence about cookies with a future tense verb?

I have the sentence
This is the best vacation I have ever had!

Who has a sentence about a baby with a future tense verb?

I have the sentence
The cookies will be ready in five minutes.

Who has a sentence about a vacation with a past tense verb?

Tenses—Past, Present, or Future?

I have the sentence
We took so many pictures of our vacation.

Who has a sentence about socks with a future tense verb?

I have the sentence
We found the lake last year while on vacation.

Who has a sentence about soccer with a future tense verb?

I have the sentence
The new socks will be ordered from the Internet company.

Who has a sentence about camping with a past tense verb?

I have the sentence
We will play your soccer team next week.

Who has a sentence about a broken arm with a present tense verb?

I have the sentence **They left early this morning to go camping.**

Who has a sentence about a table with a future tense verb?

I have the sentence
The doctor is placing the boy's broken arm in a cast.

Who has a sentence about a picnic with a future tense verb?

I have the sentence
The table will be used for the family dinner.

Who has a sentence about a turtle with a present tense verb?

I have the sentence
Will our next door neighbors go on the picnic too?

Who has a sentence about camping with a present tense verb?

I have the sentence **Look! Is that really a turtle trying to cross the road?**

Who has a sentence about a lake with a past tense verb?

I have the sentence
Are you enjoying your first camping trip?

Who has a sentence about fruit with a present tense verb?

Tenses—Past, Present, or Future?

I have the sentence
Please pass the apples.

Who has a sentence about rabbits with a future tense verb?

I have the sentence
The lake will be closed for the winter.

Who has a sentence about a table with a present tense verb?

I have the sentence
The baby rabbits should be born in the next few days.

Who has a sentence about a picnic with a past tense verb?

I have the sentence
The table looks so lovely tonight.

Who has a sentence about socks with a present tense verb?

I have the sentence
The ants were all over the picnic table!

Who has a sentence about a baby with a present tense verb?

I have the sentence **Both of my socks have holes in them!**

Who has a sentence about a turtle with a future tense verb?

I have a sentence
My baby is a girl.

Who has a sentence about cookies with a past tense verb?

I have the sentence
The turtle should cross the road by noon.

Who has a sentence about soccer with a past tense verb?

I have the sentence
She accidentally burned the cookies.

Who has a sentence about a lake with a future tense verb?

I have the sentence
My team won the soccer game.

Who has the first card?

Tenses—Past, Present, or Future?

Follow the path by highlighting the sentences as your classmates identify them.

We have seven pet rabbits.	He broke his arm when he fell off the mountain.	The cookies will be ready in five minutes.
The apples were picked last week.	She went shopping last night.	We took so many pictures of our vacation.
Will your baby be a boy or a girl?	This is the best vacation I have ever had!	The new socks will be ordered from the Internet company.
The turtle won the race.	You will break your arm if you climb that mountain!	They left early this morning to go camping.
Why are there so many ants here?	They will be coming home from the camping trip.	The table will be used for the family dinner.
The waves on the lake are so smooth.	It all started three months ago with two rabbits.	Look! Is that really a turtle trying to cross the road?
The oranges will be ripe in two weeks.	The leg of the table broke during dinner.	We found the lake last year while on vacation.
Start *	Are the cookies burning?	We will play your soccer team next week.
The baby cried.	I lost my socks last week at camp.	The doctor is placing the boy's broken arm in a cast.
They are playing soccer at the park.	I will be leaving for my vacation next week.	Will our next door neighbors go on the picnic too?
Where will your cruise ship go?	This hamburger is delicious.	Are you enjoying your first camping trip?
The ants were all over the picnic table!	The baby rabbits should be born in the next few days.	Please pass the apples.
My baby is a girl.	She accidentally burned the cookies.	I am working on my project.
She ate all of her vegetables.	The lake will be closed for the winter.	We will go to the zoo tomorrow.
Both of my socks have holes in them!	The table looks so lovely tonight.	They donated cans to the food bank.
The turtle should cross the road by noon.	**Finish** * My team won the soccer game.	They will be eating at the restaurant around the corner.

Look at the boxes you did **not** highlight. Write the tense of the verb in each remaining sentence in order from left to right.

1. ________________ 2. ________________ 3. ________________ 4. ________________

5. ________________ 6. ________________ 7. ________________ 8. ________________

Prefixes and Suffixes

I have the **first card.**

Who has the prefix in *automatic*?

I have **post-, which means "after."**

Who has the prefix in *bicycle*?

I have **auto-, which means "self."**

Who has the prefix in *interact*?

I have **bi-, which means "two."**

Who has the prefix in *sympathy*?

I have **inter-, which means "between."**

Who has the prefix in *depart*?

I have **sym-, which means "together."**

Who has the prefix in *disagree*?

I have **de-, which means "from."**

Who has the prefix in *export*?

I have **dis-, which means "not."**

Who has the prefix in *biology*?

I have **ex-, which means "out."**

Who has the prefix in *postpone*?

I have **bio-, which means "life."**

Who has the prefix in *unhappy*?

Prefixes and Suffixes

I have **un-, which means "not."**

Who has the prefix in *irregular*?

I have **sub-, which means "under."**

Who has the prefix in *contradict*?

I have **ir-, which means "not."**

Who has the prefix in *polygon*?

I have **contra-, which means "against."**

Who has the prefix in *malnutrition*?

I have **poly-, which means "many."**

Who has the prefix in *monopoly*?

I have **mal-, which means "bad."**

Who has the prefix in *telephone*?

I have **mono-, which means "one."**

Who has the prefix in *microscope*?

I have **tele-, which means "at a distance."**

Who has the prefix in *recall*?

I have **micro-, which means "small."**

Who has the prefix in *submarine*?

I have **re-, which means "again."**

Who has the prefix in *transport*?

Prefixes and Suffixes

I have **trans-, which means "across."**

Who has the prefix in *preview*?

I have **mis-, which means "wrong."**

Who has the prefix in *imperfect*?

I have **pre-, which means "before."**

Who has the prefix in *photograph*?

I have **im-, which means "not."**

Who has the prefix in *triangle*?

I have **photo-, which means "produced by light."**

Who has the prefix in *indirect*?

I have **tri-, which means "three."**

Who has the prefix in *coexist*?

I have **in-, which means "not."**

Who has the prefix in *obstruct*?

I have **co-, which means "together."**

Who has the prefix in *supervisor*?

I have **ob-, which means "against."**

Who has the prefix in *misunderstanding*?

I have **super-, which means "above."**

Who has the prefix in *centimeter?*

Prefixes and Suffixes

I have **centi-, which means "hundred."**

Who has the suffix in *comfortable*?

I have -**ist, which means "one who does something."**

Who has the suffix in *arachnaphobia*?

I have -**able, which means "able to be" or "capable."**

Who has the suffix in *doctor*?

I have **-phobia, which means "fear of."**

Who has the suffix in *hardest*?

I have -**or, which means "a person who does something."**

Who has the suffix in *biology*?

I have -**est, which means "the highest when comparing things."**

Who has the suffix in *beautify*?

I have **-ology, which means "the study of something."**

Who has the suffix in *careless*?

I have -**ify, which means "to make."**

Who has the suffix in *teacher*?

I have **-less, which means "without."**

Who has the suffix in *artist*?

I have -**er, which means "one who does something."**

Who has the first card?

Prefixes and Suffixes

Write the prefix or suffix for each word in the boxes below from left to right as your classmates identify the answers.

START →			
A	B	C	D

Write the prefixes and suffixes from Column D. Match each prefix and suffix with its meaning from the box below.

from
together
under
one who does something
not
three
not
one who does something
again
capable, able to be

1. ____________ means ____________
2. ____________ means ____________
3. ____________ means ____________
4. ____________ means ____________
5. ____________ means ____________
6. ____________ means ____________
7. ____________ means ____________
8. ____________ means ____________
9. ____________ means ____________
10. ____________ means ____________

Greek and Latin Roots

I have the **first card**.

Who has the root in *retrospect*?

I have ***ject,* which means "to throw."**

Who has the root in *repel*?

I have ***spect,* which means "to see."**

Who has the root in *parasol?*

I have ***pel,* which means "to drive."**

Who has the root in *import*?

I have ***sol,* which means "sun."**

Who has the root in *predict*?

I have ***port,* which means "to carry."**

Who has the root in *describe*?

I have ***dict,* which means "to say."**

Who has the root in *progress*?

I have ***scribe,* which means "to write."**

Who has the root in *extract*?

I have ***gress,* which means "to walk."**

Who has the root in *inject*?

I have ***tract,* which means "to pull."**

Who has the root in *divert*?

Greek and Latin Roots

I have ***vert,* which means**
"to turn."

Who has the root in *pendulum*?

I have ***chron,* which means**
"time."

Who has the root in *philharmonic*?

I have ***pend,* which means**
"to hang."

Who has the root in *monochrome*?

I have ***phil,* which means**
"to love."

Who has the root in *sympathy*?

I have ***chrome,* which means**
"color."

Who has the root in *democracy*?

I have ***path,* which means**
"feeling" or "suffering."

Who has the root in *audible*?

I have ***dem,* which means**
"people."

Who has the root in *phonics*?

I have ***audi,* which means**
"to hear."

Who has the root in *transmit*?

I have ***phon,* which means**
"sound."

Who has the root in *chronicle*?

I have ***mit,* which means**
"to send."

Who has the root in *fracture*?

Greek and Latin Roots

I have ***fract,* which means "break."**

Who has the root in *remember*?

I have ***cent,* which means "one hundred."**

Who has the root in *visor*?

I have ***mem,* which means "keep in mind."**

Who has the root in *pedestrian*?

I have ***vis,* which means "to see."**

Who has the root in *thermos*?

I have ***ped,* which means "foot."**

Who has the root in *liberate*?

I have ***therm,* which means "heat."**

Who has the root in *astronaut*?

I have ***liber,* which means "to free."**

Who has the root in *creation*?

I have ***astro,* which means "stars" or "space."**

Who has the root in *paragraph*?

I have ***creat,* which means "to make."**

Who has the root in *percent*?

I have ***graph,* which means "writing."**

Who has the root in *conjunction*?

Greek and Latin Roots

I have ***junc,*** **which means “to join.”**

Who has the root in *dermatologist*?

I have ***par,*** **which means “equality.”**

Who has the root in *vital*?

I have ***derm,*** **which means “skin.”**

Who has the root in *ambidextrous*?

I have ***vit,*** **which means “life.”**

Who has the root in *telescope*?

I have ***ambi,*** **which means “both.”**

Who has the root in *monarchy*?

I have ***tele,*** **which means “far away.”**

Who has the root in *vacuum*?

I have ***arch,*** **which means “rule.”**

Who has the root in *juror*?

I have ***vac,*** **which means “empty.”**

Who has the root in *volunteer*?

I have ***jur,*** **which means “law” or “justice.”**

Who has the root in *compare*?

I have ***vol,*** **which means “will.”**

Who has the first card?

Greek and Latin Roots

As your classmates identify the answers, write the root for each word in the boxes below from left to right and top to bottom.

START →			
A	B	C	D

List the roots from Column B. Match each root with its meaning from the box below.

to throw
far away
one hundred
rule
people
feeling or suffering
writing
to pull
keep in mind
to see

1. ____________________ means ____________________

2. ____________________ means ____________________

3. ____________________ means ____________________

4. ____________________ means ____________________

5. ____________________ means ____________________

6. ____________________ means ____________________

7. ____________________ means ____________________

8. ____________________ means ____________________

9. ____________________ means ____________________

10. ____________________ means ____________________

Base Words

I have the **first card**.

Who has the base word in *unbelievable*?

I have **test**.

Who has the base word in *cooperate*?

I have **believe**.

Who has the base word in *biweekly*?

I have **operate**.

Who has the base word in *abnormal*?

I have **week**.

Who has the base word in *unopened*?

I have **normal**.

Who has the base word in *unicycle*?

I have **open**.

Who has the base word in *misunderstanding*?

I have **cycle**.

Who has the base word in *bravest*?

I have **understand**.

Who has the base word in *pretest*?

I have **brave**.

Who has the base word in *driven*?

Base Words

I have **drive**.

Who has the base word in *arrived*?

I have **migrate**.

Who has the base word in *prejudge*?

I have **arrive**.

Who has the base word in *strongest*?

I have **judge**.

Who has the base word in *redirect*?

I have **strong**.

Who has the base word in *cracking*?

I have **direct**.

Who has the base word in *enlighten*?

I have **crack**.

Who has the base word in *smartest*?

I have **light**.

Who has the base word in *displease*?

I have **smart**.

Who has the base word in *migration*?

I have **please**.

Who has the base word in *antitoxin*?

Base Words

I have **toxin**.

Who has the base word in *automobile*?

I have **throne**.

Who has the base word in *reappear*?

I have **mobile**.

Who has the base word in *defrost*?

I have **appear**.

Who has the base word in *triangle*?

I have **frost**.

Who has the base word in *exchange*?

I have **angle**.

Who has the base word in *unhappy*?

I have **change**.

Who has the base word in *interact*?

I have **happy**.

Who has the base word in *prepaid*?

I have **act**.

Who has the base word in *enthrone*?

I have **paid**.

Who has the base word in *misspell*?

Base Words

I have **spell**.

Who has the base word in *imperfect*?

I have **refuse**.

Who has the base word in *baker*?

I have **perfect**.

Who has the base word in *refresh*?

I have **bake**.

Who has the base word in *wisdom*?

I have **fresh**.

Who has the base word in *submarine*?

I have **wise**.

Who has the base word in *dependent*?

I have **marine**.

Who has the base word in *empower*?

I have **depend**.

Who has the base word in *worker*?

I have **power**.

Who has the base word in *refusal*?

I have **work**.

Who has the first card?

Base Words

As your classmates identify the answers, highlight the letters that spell each base word. Each new word is near the previous word. Words do not share letters and do not go backwards or diagonally. Clue: The first word is in the twelfth row.

M	T	P	A	J	U	D	G	E	M	I	G	R	A	T	E	D	O	W
O	O	L	D	I	R	E	C	T	S	C	A	E	I	B	A	K	E	I
B	X	E	L	D	A	T	E	A	M	R	R	E	F	U	S	E	M	S
I	I	A	I	A	G	R	E	E	A	A	U	P	O	W	E	R	A	E
L	N	S	G	A	E	I	A	U	R	C	S	T	R	O	N	G	R	D
E	F	E	H	H	A	P	P	Y	T	K	A	R	R	I	V	E	I	E
A	R	A	T	U	N	D	E	R	S	T	A	N	D	A	E	D	N	P
P	O	A	E	O	P	E	N	W	A	T	E	S	T	A	E	R	E	E
P	S	C	H	A	N	G	E	E	O	P	E	R	A	T	E	I	F	N
E	T	A	C	T	I	I	O	E	E	N	O	R	M	A	L	V	R	D
A	T	H	R	O	N	E	A	K	E	P	C	Y	C	L	E	E	E	W
R	A	B	E	L	I	E	V	E	A	A	A	B	R	A	V	E	S	O
A	N	G	L	E	H	A	P	P	Y	I	S	P	E	L	L	A	H	R
O	U	C	O	M	F	O	R	T	U	D	P	E	R	F	E	C	T	K

The following base words are also hidden in the word search. Locate each word and then add a prefix, suffix, or root to it to create a new word.

1. date ______________________

2. do ______________________

3. agree ______________________

4. happy ______________________

5. comfort ______________________

HINT: If you did everything correctly, all the remaining letters are vowels.

Alphabetical Order

I have the **first card**.

Who has the word that comes first in alphabetical order: barley, backbone, bat?

I have **backbone**.

Who has the word that comes first in alphabetical order: bat, barn, bag?

I have **bag**.

Who has the word that comes first in alphabetical order: declare, dog, dare?

I have **dare**.

Who has the word that comes first in alphabetical order: dog, donut, doll?

I have **dog**.

Who has the word that comes first in alphabetical order: mill, mend, more?

I have **mend**.

Who has the word that comes first in alphabetical order: shelf, stove, shell?

I have **shelf**.

Who has the word that comes first in alphabetical order: lack, lady, law?

I have **lack**.

Who has the word that comes first in alphabetical order: fudge, false, feed?

I have **false**.

Who has the word that comes first in alphabetical order: mud, move, more?

I have **more**.

Who has the word that comes first in alphabetical order: shovel, shell, shin?

Alphabetical Order

I have **shell**.

Who has the word that comes first in alphabetical order: cover, code, cup?

I have **mill**.

Who has the word that comes first in alphabetical order: loft, lunch, love?

I have **code**.

Who has the word that comes first in alphabetical order: loft, law, lift?

I have **loft**.

Who has the word that comes first in alphabetical order: drip, drop, dent?

I have **law**.

Who has the word that comes first in alphabetical order: stove, supper, stunt?

I have **dent**.

Who has the word that comes first in alphabetical order: fought, fight, fine?

I have **stove**.

Who has the word that comes first in alphabetical order: felt, feed, fight?

I have **fight**.

Who has the word that comes first in alphabetical order: cup, cover, cut?

I have **feed**.

Who has the word that comes first in alphabetical order: mitt, mill, miss?

I have **cover**.

Who has the word that comes first in alphabetical order: dull, drip, drove?

Alphabetical Order

I have **drip**.

Who has the word that comes first in alphabetical order: lodge, long, lunge?

I have **waste**.

Who has the word that comes first in alphabetical order: like, lift, little?

I have **lodge**.

Who has the word that comes first in alphabetical order: clap, chew, crate?

I have **lift**.

Who has the word that comes first in alphabetical order: guard, garden, glue?

I have **chew**.

Who has the word that comes first in alphabetical order: tower, toe, tray?

I have **garden**.

Who has the word that comes first in alphabetical order: tray, treat, trunk?

I have **toe**.

Who has the word that comes first in alphabetical order: happy, hip, hat?

I have **tray**.

Who has the word that comes first in alphabetical order: wheat, water, world?

I have **happy**.

Who has the word that comes first in alphabetical order: water, waste, white?

I have **water**.

Who has the word that comes first in alphabetical order: lung, long, loop?

Alphabetical Order

I have **long**.

Who has the word that comes first in alphabetical order: coat, clap, coast?

I have **jar**.

Who has the word that comes first in alphabetical order: chat, chase, choose?

I have **clap**.

Who has the word that comes first in alphabetical order: trust, treat, trim?

I have **chase**.

Who has the word that comes first in alphabetical order: white, wheat, wool?

I have **treat**.

Who has the word that comes first in alphabetical order: goat, glue, gust?

I have **wheat**.

Who has the word that comes first in alphabetical order: choose, chunk, chore?

I have **glue**.

Who has the word that comes first in alphabetical order: hunt, hip, hop?

I have **choose**.

Who has the word that comes first in alphabetical order: joke, junk, jolly?

I have **hip**.

Who has the word that comes first in alphabetical order: jar, joke, jug?

I have **joke**.

Who has the first card?

Alphabetical Order

Follow the path by highlighting the answers as your classmates identify them.

LACK	FALSE	MORE	SHELL	DARK	DRIP	LODGE	CHEW
SHELF	MEND	DOG	CODE	COVER	SMILE	HAPPY	TOE
BARLEY	RANGE	DARE	LAW	PART	FIGHT	WASTE	SCARE
START *	BACKBONE	BAG	STOVE	LOFT	DENT	LIFT	GARDEN
HEAD	MUTTER	RAPID	FEED	MILL	CLEAN	WATER	TRAY
JOKE	CHOOSE	WHEAT	CHEF	HIP	GLUE	PLANE	LONG
FINISH *	GIRL	CASE	CHASE	JAR	ORANGE	TREAT	CLAP

Look at the boxes you did **not** highlight. Write the words in these boxes in alphabetical order.

Rhyme Time 1

I have the **first card**.

Who has the word that rhymes with *maid*?

I have **divided**.

Who has the word that rhymes with *trim*?

I have **played**.

Who has the word that rhymes with *spent*?

I have **grim**.

Who has the word that rhymes with *attending*?

I have **represent**.

Who has the word that rhymes with *shook*?

I have **lending**.

Who has the word that rhymes with *speech*?

I have **brook**.

Who has the word that rhymes with *essential*?

I have **each**.

Who has the word that rhymes with *throat*?

I have **residential**.

Who has the word that rhymes with *decided*?

I have **promote**.

Who has the word that rhymes with *duty*?

Rhyme Time 1

I have **beauty**.

Who has the word that rhymes with *sweep*?

I have **dew**.

Who has the word that rhymes with *request*?

I have **sheep**.

Who has the word that rhymes with *learn*?

I have **pressed**.

Who has the word that rhymes with *cotton*?

I have **concern**.

Who has the word that rhymes with *rough*?

I have **forgotten**.

Who has the word that rhymes with *knees*?

I have **puff**.

Who has the word that rhymes with *wool*?

I have **sneeze**.

Who has the word that rhymes with *hurt*?

I have **full**.

Who has the word that rhymes with *view*?

I have **convert**.

Who has the word that rhymes with *knee*?

Rhyme Time 1

I have **disagree**.

Who has the word that rhymes with *round*?

I have **dizzy**.

Who has the word that rhymes with *vault*?

I have **astound**.

Who has the word that rhymes with *dollar*?

I have **default**.

Who has the word that rhymes with *gear*?

I have **scholar**.

Who has the word that rhymes with *murky*?

I have **souvenir**.

Who has the word that rhymes with *smarter*?

I have **turkey**.

Who has the word that rhymes with *worry*?

I have **charter**.

Who has the word that rhymes with *shirt*?

I have **hurry**.

Who has the word that rhymes with *busy*?

I have **squirt**.

Who has the word that rhymes with *sleeve*?

Rhyme Time 1

I have **deceive**.

Who has the word that rhymes with *trail*?

I have **caboose**.

Who has the word that rhymes with *legal*?

I have **inhale**.

Who has the word that rhymes with *partake*?

I have **eagle**.

Who has the word that rhymes with *invention*?

I have **shake**.

Who has the word that rhymes with *harsh*?

I have **attention**.

Who has the word that rhymes with *bleacher*?

I have **marsh**.

Who has the word that rhymes with *master*?

I have **creature**.

Who has the word that rhymes with *prune*?

I have **disaster**.

Who has the word that rhymes with *juice*?

I have **baboon**.

Who has the first card?

Rhyme Time 1

Fill in the missing letters of the rhyming words as your classmates identify them. Start at the arrow and go from left to right and top to bottom.

START →	_ _ A _ _ _	_ E _ _ E _ _ _ _ _	_ _ O O _
_ E _ I _ E _ _ I A _	_ I _ I _ E _	_ _ I _	_ E _ _ _ _ _ _
_ A _ _	_ _ O _ O _ _	_ E A U _ _	_ _ E _ _
_ O _ C E _ _	_ U _ _	_ U _ _	_ E W
_ _ E _ _ _ _ _	_ O _ _ O _ _ E _	_ _ E E _ _	_ O _ _ E _ _
_ I _ A _ _ _ _ _	A _ T O U _ _	_ C H O _ A _	_ U _ K _ _
_ U _ _ _	_ I _ _ Y	_ E F A U _ _	_ O U _ E _ I R
_ _ A R _ _ _	_ _ U I _ _	_ E C E I _ _	I _ _ A _ _
S _ _ K _	_ A _ _ _	_ I _ A _ _ _ _ _	_ A _ O O _ E
E A _ _ _	A _ _ E _ T _ _ _	_ _ E A _ U R _	_ A _ O O _
A	**B**	**C**	**D**

List the words from Column C. Write at least one rhyming word for each word.

1. ____________________ rhymes with ____________________
2. ____________________ rhymes with ____________________
3. ____________________ rhymes with ____________________
4. ____________________ rhymes with ____________________
5. ____________________ rhymes with ____________________
6. ____________________ rhymes with ____________________
7. ____________________ rhymes with ____________________
8. ____________________ rhymes with ____________________
9. ____________________ rhymes with ____________________
10. ____________________ rhymes with ____________________

Rhyme Time 2

I have the **first card**.

Who has a clever organ?

I have **cross sauce**.

Who has a tardy argument?

I have a **smart heart**.

Who has a unique duo?

I have a **late debate**.

Who has an animal trainer?

I have a **rare pair**.

Who has sleepy wood?

I have a **creature teacher**.

Who has the sea's magic formula?

I have **slumber lumber**.

Who has an unhappy father?

I have an **ocean potion**.

Who has a group of fuzzy letters?

I have a **sad dad**.

Who has angry gravy?

I have a **blurred word**.

Who has icy metal?

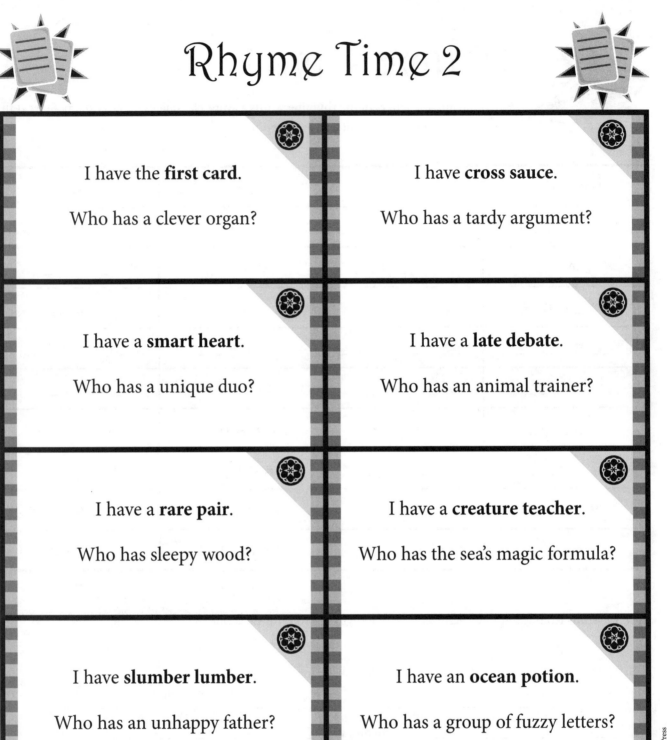

Rhyme Time 2

I have **cold gold**. Who has a torn play?	I have a **thrown stone**. Who has a joking cloth?
I have a **ripped script**. Who has a speedy present?	I have a **gag rag**. Who has a hurting entrance?
I have a **swift gift**. Who has a pleasing rhythm?	I have a **sore door**. Who has an unhappy boy?
I have a **neat beat**. Who has a magical iguana?	I have a **sad lad**. Who has a tardy worm?
I have a **wizard lizard**. Who has a tossed pebble?	I have **late bait**. Who has a sugary steak?

Rhyme Time 2

I have **sweet meat**.

Who has a dark bag?

I have **city pity**.

Who has a terrific musical group?

I have a **black sack**.

Who has a nightmare sound?

I have a **grand band**.

Who has a mean sword fight?

I have a **dream scream**.

Who has bathing time?

I have a **cruel duel**.

Who has an empty bird?

I have **shower hour**.

Who has an obese feline?

I have a **hollow swallow**.

Who has a tiny hive dweller?

I have a **fat cat**.

Who has a big town's sympathy?

I have a **wee bee**.

Who has a gooey robbery?

Rhyme Time 2

I have a **slime crime**.

Who has a tidy female monarch?

I have a **brave save**.

Who has a rodent home?

I have a **clean queen**.

Who has a fiery pan?

I have a **mouse house**.

Who has a red facial part?

I have a **hot pot**.

Who has a diamond's energy?

I have a **rose nose**.

Who has a wet light?

I have **jewel fuel**.

Who has the broken truth?

I have a **damp lamp**.

Who has a dark sign?

I have the **cracked fact**.

Who has a courageous rescue?

I have a **black plaque**.

Who has the first card?

Rhyme Time 2

Follow the path by highlighting the rhyming words as your classmates identify them.

FUNNY MONEY	CLEAN QUEEN	HOT POT	JEWEL FUEL	MOWED ROAD
WEE BEE	SLIME CRIME	BRAVE SAVE	CRACKED FACT	FINISH* BLACK PLAQUE
HOLLOW SWALLOW	CRUEL DUEL	MOUSE HOUSE	ROSE NOSE	DAMP LAMP
BEAR STARE	GRAND BAND	SHOWER HOUR	DREAM SCREAM	BLACK SACK
START *	CITY PITY	FAT CAT	GLAD PAD	SWEET MEAT
SMART HEART	SQUID KID	GHOST TOAST	NOODLE POODLE	LATE BAIT
RARE PAIR	RIPPED SCRIPT	SWIFT GIFT	NEAT BEAT	SAD LAD
SLUMBER LUMBER	COLD GOLD	BLURRED WORD	WIZARD LIZARD	SORE DOOR
SAD DAD	BOOK COOK	OCEAN POTION	THROWN STONE	GAG RAG
CROSS SAUCE	LATE DEBATE	CREATURE TEACHER	BLESSED TEST	PLAIN TRAIN

Look at the boxes you did **not** highlight. Choose five pairs of rhyming words. Create your own riddle for each pair of words. Be creative. Draw pictures on the back of this paper to show how the answers might look.

1. ______________________________

2. ______________________________

3. ______________________________

4. ______________________________

5. ______________________________

Multiple-Meaning Words 1

I have the **first card**.

Who has a sentence with *pet* used differently than in this sentence:
I have a pet rabbit.

I have the sentence
It's time for a lunch break.

Who has a sentence with *point* used differently than in this sentence:
That pencil has a very sharp point.

I have the sentence
We like to pet puppies.

Who has a sentence with *post* used differently than in this sentence:
My teacher will post the grades on the door.

I have the sentence
It's rude to point at people.

Who has a sentence with *crack* used differently than in this sentence:
There was a crack in the ceiling.

I have the sentence
He pounded the post deep into the ground.

Who has a sentence with *pack* used differently than in this sentence:
The pack of wolves was sleeping.

I have the sentence
I'll help you crack the walnuts.

Who has a sentence with *taste* used differently than in this sentence:
You have terrific taste in furniture.

I have the sentence
I need to pack my suitcase for the trip.

Who has a sentence with *color* used differently than in this sentence:
Blue is my favorite color.

I have the sentence
How does the pasta taste?

Who has a sentence with *spring* used differently than in this sentence:
I broke the spring on this trampoline.

I have the sentence
She will color her hair light pink.

Who has a sentence with *break* used differently than in this sentence:
What did you break now?

I have the sentence
It's time to spring out of bed!

Who has a sentence with *place* used differently than in this sentence:
Please place your homework in the basket.

Multiple-Meaning Words 1

I have the sentence
Where is his new place located?

Who has a sentence with *store* used differently than in this sentence:
This new box is where you'll store your toys.

I have the sentence
I taught my ferret how to roll over.

Who has a sentence with *master* used differently than in this sentence:
He is a master at scientific experiments.

I have the sentence
It's time to go to the grocery store.

Who has a sentence with *snap* used differently than in this sentence:
The snap on my jacket is broken.

I have the sentence
It takes hard work to master a skill.

Who has a sentence with *report* used differently than in this sentence:
Your report is due Monday.

I have the sentence
I'll have your car repaired in a snap.

Who has a sentence with *raise* used differently than in this sentence:
She asked her boss for a raise.

I have the sentence
You need to report your grades to your mother.

Who has a sentence with *cut* used differently than in this sentence:
We cut out the pictures from that magazine.

I have the sentence
Who would like to raise the flag?

Who has a sentence with *fool* used differently than in this sentence:
It's not nice to fool your little sister.

I have the sentence
He had a cut on his toe.

Who has a sentence with *fire* used differently than in this sentence:
The manager had to fire the lazy employee.

I have the sentence
I acted like such a fool.

Who has a sentence with *roll* used differently than in this sentence:
Would you like butter for your roll?

I have the sentence
Where is the wood for the fire?

Who has a sentence with *shape* used differently than in this sentence:
This shape is a hexagon.

Multiple-Meaning Words 1

I have the sentence
Cara tried to shape the clay into a vase.

Who has a sentence with *track* used differently than in this sentence:
He was trying to track how much money he spent each month.

I have the sentence
The boat was supposed to float.

Who has a sentence with *post* used differently than in this sentence:
Joey pounded the post into the dirt.

I have the sentence
They ran three laps around the track.

Who has a sentence with *bend* used differently than in this sentence:
Her house was just around the bend in the road.

I have the sentence
Mr. Jones will post the grades.

Who has a sentence with *soil* used differently than in this sentence:
Try not to soil your new clothes during recess.

I have the sentence
Try not to bend the edges of the book.

Who has a sentence with *corner* used differently than in this sentence:
In the wild, some animals try to corner their prey.

I have the sentence
The roses grew tall in the potting soil.

Who has a sentence with *string* used differently than in this sentence:
The guitar string broke.

I have the sentence
Her desk was in the corner of her room.

Who has a sentence with *shine* used differently than in this sentence:
There was a shine on the car window because it was so clean.

I have the sentence
Mia has to string beads to make a necklace.

Who has a sentence with *pumps* used differently than in this sentence:
Tina's mom bought a new pair of pumps to match her suit.

I have the sentence
Would you like me to shine your shoes?

Who has a sentence with *float* used differently than in this sentence:
Maria asked for a root beer float.

I have the sentence
The water pumps are out of order.

Who has a sentence with *brush* used differently than in this sentence:
I bought a hair brush.

Multiple-Meaning Words 1

I have the sentence
You should brush your teeth every day.

Who has a sentence with *bowl* used differently than in this sentence:
I want to have a birthday party where we can bowl.

I have the sentence
I trust you to keep a secret.

Who has a sentence with *root* used differently than in this sentence:
You need to get to the root of the problem.

I have the sentence
I placed a bowl of fruit on the table.

Who has a sentence with *patch* used differently than in this sentence:
Do you see that patch of roses over there?

I have the sentence
It's time to root for your favorite team.

Who has a sentence with *fast* used differently than in this sentence:
He had to fast for 24 hours before his operation.

I have the sentence
I need a tailor to patch these jeans.

Who has a sentence with *share* used differently than in this sentence:
Pam bought a share of stock in her favorite company.

I have the sentence
Look at how fast he can pitch!

Who has a sentence with *bat* used differently than in this sentence:
A baseball player needs a good bat.

I have the sentence
Will you share those cookies with me?

Who has a sentence with *mouse* used differently than in this sentence:
Jenna bought a new wireless mouse for her laptop.

I have the sentence
A bat flew out of the cave.

Who has a sentence with *tip* used differently than in this sentence:
Luis gave a good tip to his barber.

I have the sentence
There was a mouse in the garage.

Who has a sentence with *trust* used differently than in this sentence:
Peter's grandma kept money in a trust fund for his college education.

I have the sentence
Try not to tip over the gameboard.

Who has the first card?

Multiple-Meaning Words 1

Follow the path by highlighting the sentences as your classmates identify them.

START *	I NEED TO PACK MY SUITCASE FOR THE TRIP.	SHE WILL COLOR HER HAIR LIGHT PINK.
WE LIKE TO PET PUPPIES.	HE POUNDED THE POST DEEP INTO THE GROUND.	IT'S TIME FOR A LUNCH BREAK.
IT'S TIME TO SPRING OUT OF BED!	HOW DOES THE PASTA TASTE?	IT'S RUDE TO POINT AT PEOPLE.
WHERE IS HIS NEW PLACE LOCATED?	IT'S TIME TO GO TO THE GROCERY STORE.	I'LL HELP YOU CRACK THE WALNUTS.
ARE YOU READY FOR ME TO DEAL THE CARDS?	I'LL HAVE YOUR CAR REPAIRED IN A SNAP.	WHO WOULD LIKE TO RAISE THE FLAG?
DID YOU DRESS THE BABY YET?	HE PUT A DARK FINISH ON THE WOOD CABINET.	I ACTED LIKE SUCH A FOOL.
THEY RAN THREE LAPS AROUND THE TRACK.	CARA TRIED TO SHAPE THE CLAY INTO A VASE.	I TAUGHT MY FERRET HOW TO ROLL OVER.
TRY NOT TO BEND THE EDGES OF THE BOOK.	WHERE IS THE WOOD FOR THE FIRE?	IT TAKES HARD WORK TO MASTER A SKILL.
HER DESK WAS IN THE CORNER OF HER ROOM.	HE HAD A CUT ON HIS TOE.	YOU NEED TO REPORT YOUR GRADES TO YOUR MOTHER.
WOULD YOU LIKE ME TO SHINE YOUR SHOES?	THE BOAT WAS SUPPOSED TO FLOAT.	IT'S SMART TO FACE YOUR FEARS.
SHE NEEDED TO FAST FOR TWO DAYS.	MR. JONES WILL POST THE GRADES.	THE ROSES GREW TALL IN THE POTTING SOIL.
YOU SHOULD BRUSH YOUR TEETH EVERY DAY.	THE WATER PUMPS ARE OUT OF ORDER.	MIA HAS TO STRING THE BEADS TO MAKE A NECKLACE.
I PLACED A BOWL OF FRUIT ON THE TABLE.	I NEED A TAILOR TO PATCH THESE JEANS.	DID YOU SET THE CHICKENS FREE?
IS THE CAR IN GEAR?	WILL YOU SHARE THOSE COOKIES WITH ME?	KEEP YOUR EYES PEELED FOR THE SIGN.
I TRUST YOU TO KEEP A SECRET.	THERE WAS A MOUSE IN THE GARAGE.	SHE TRIED TO REASON WITH HER FATHER.
IT'S TIME TO ROOT FOR YOUR FAVORITE TEAM.	THE SHIRT WAS WRINKLED, SO SHE NEEDED TO PRESS IT.	PLEASE PLAY THAT NOTE ON YOUR PIANO.
LOOK AT HOW FAST HE CAN PITCH!	A BAT FLEW OUT OF THE CAVE.	FINISH * TRY NOT TO TIP OVER THE GAMEBOARD.

Look at the boxes you did **not** highlight. Write the multiple-meaning word in each sentence.

1. ____________ **4.** ____________ **7.** ____________ **10.** ____________

2. ____________ **5.** ____________ **8.** ____________ **11.** ____________

3. ____________ **6.** ____________ **9.** ____________

Multiple-Meaning Words 2

I have the **first card**.

Who has a sentence with *accent* used differently than in this sentence: His accent was very European.

I have the sentence **Did you flush the toilet?**

Who has a sentence with *game* used differently than in this sentence: They hunted game in the forest.

I have the sentence **I like how you chose to accent the colors in your bedspread.**

Who has a sentence with *change* used differently than in this sentence: How much change is in your wallet?

I have the sentence **Which game would you like to play first?**

Who has a sentence with *face* used differently than in this sentence: You need to face your fears.

I have the sentence **You need to change your shoes.**

Who has a sentence with *free* used differently than in this sentence: The court decided to free the man.

I have the sentence **The baby has applesauce all over his face.**

Who has a sentence with *find* used differently than in this sentence: She knew it was a good find at the closeout sale.

I have the sentence **The sign said, "Buy one, get one free."**

Who has a sentence with *form* used differently than in this sentence: Write your name on this line of the form.

I have the sentence **Can you find the street on the map?**

Who has a sentence with *application* used differently than in this sentence: He filled out the job application.

I have the sentence **You can form the line right here.**

Who has a sentence with *flush* used differently than in this sentence: Her face began to flush and turn red.

I have the sentence **You only need one application of shampoo to wash your hair.**

Who has a sentence with *fan* used differently than in this sentence: The fan kept them cool.

Multiple-Meaning Words 2

I have the sentence
Are you a sports fan?

Who has a sentence with *knocked* used differently than in this sentence: Steve knocked over the display of canned food in the store.

I have the sentence
Will you please load the dryer for me?

Who has a sentence with *meet* used differently than in this sentence: They went to the track meet.

I have the sentence
She knocked on the door.

Who has a sentence with *interest* used differently than in this sentence: The scary movie sure kept his interest.

I have the sentence
I'll meet you at the theater at 8:00.

Who has a sentence with *organ* used differently than in this sentence: The ear is your hearing organ.

I have the sentence **Your bank account earns interest every month.**

Who has a sentence with *mine* used differently than in this sentence: My uncle worked in a diamond mine.

I have the sentence
Grandma plays the organ on Sundays.

Who has a sentence with *squash* used differently than in this sentence: He loves to eat squash.

I have the sentence
That jacket is mine.

Who has a sentence with *litter* used differently than in this sentence: There is a litter of puppies next door.

I have the sentence
Did you squash that bug?

Who has a sentence with *work* used differently than in this sentence: The bicycle does not work properly.

I have the sentence
The litter was thrown away.

Who has a sentence with *load* used differently than in this sentence: What a heavy load you are trying to lift.

I have the sentence
It was time to go to work.

Who has a sentence with *temples* used differently than in this sentence: I rub my temples when I have a headache.

Multiple-Meaning Words 2

I have the sentence
They saw many temples on their vacation.

Who has a sentence with *stuff* used differently than in this sentence:
What is all this stuff in your desk?

I have the sentence
She wore a pink slip under her dress.

Who has a sentence with *trace* used differently than in this sentence:
It vanished without a trace.

I have the sentence
Try not to stuff it all inside.

Who has a sentence with *wash* used differently than in this sentence:
The load of wash is almost dry.

I have the sentence
You can trace over each detail carefully.

Who has a sentence with *stand* used differently than in this sentence:
Stand up straight and tall.

I have the sentence
We need to wash the car.

Who has a sentence with *ticks* used differently than in this sentence:
The unlucky dog was full of ticks.

I have the sentence
I put the new TV stand over there.

Who has a sentence with *tend* used differently than in this sentence:
The farmer needed to tend to his sheep.

I have the sentence
The sound of the clock's ticks drove her crazy.

Who has a sentence with *wave* used differently than in this sentence:
The wave almost knocked her over.

I have the sentence
I tend to spend too much money.

Who has a sentence with *range* used differently than in this sentence:
The range of numbers is the difference between the highest and lowest numbers.

I have the sentence
Did you wave goodbye to your friend?

Who has a sentence with *slip* used differently than in this sentence:
He tried not to slip on the waxed floor.

I have the sentence
She boiled the water on her cooktop range.

Who has a sentence with *stamp* used differently than in this sentence:
I put a postage stamp on the envelope.

Multiple-Meaning Words 2

I have the sentence
Mrs. Brown will stamp each student's paper.

Who has a sentence with *matter* used differently than in this sentence:
All matter takes up space.

I have the sentence
Where did you park your car?

Who has a sentence with *tag* used differently than in this sentence:
Let's go outside and play tag.

I have the sentence
What's the matter with you today?

Who has a sentence with *lock* used differently than in this sentence:
Her mother saved a lock of hair from his first haircut.

I have the sentence
What does the price tag say?

Who has a sentence with *season* used differently than in this sentence:
Which is your favorite season?

I have the sentence **Remember to lock the door when you leave.**

Who has a sentence with *page* used differently than in this sentence:
The principal tried to page Mrs. Gomez over the intercom.

I have the sentence
First, he had to season the ribs with barbecue sauce.

Who has a sentence with *watch* used differently than in this sentence:
I can tell time with my new watch.

I have the sentence **What page are you on in your new book?**

Who has a sentence with *mold* used differently than in this sentence:
There was mold on the bread.

I have the sentence
We can watch television after dinner.

Who has a sentence with *well* used differently than in this sentence:
You did well on your math test.

I have the sentence
She tried to mold the dough into a loaf of bread.

Who has a sentence with *park* used differently than in this sentence:
They loved feeding the ducks at the park.

I have the sentence
They had to dig a well to get water for their country house.

Who has the first card?

Multiple-Meaning Words 2

Follow the path by highlighting the sentences as your classmates identify them.

What is the make of your new car?	Where did you park your car?	What does the price tag say?	**Finish** * They had to dig a well to get water for their country house.
What page are you on in your new book?	She tried to mold the dough into a loaf of bread.	First, he had to season the ribs with barbecue sauce.	We can watch television after dinner.
Remember to lock the door when you leave.	What's the matter with you today?	She put strawberry preserves on her toast.	How would you rate that book on a scale of 1 to 5?
She boiled the water on her cooktop range.	Mrs. Brown will stamp each student's paper.	The sound of the clock's ticks drove her crazy.	We need to wash the car.
I tend to spend too much money.	She wore a pink slip under her dress.	Did you wave goodbye to your friend?	Try not to stuff it all inside.
I put the new TV stand over there.	You can trace over each detail carefully.	The final pass led to a touchdown.	They saw many temples on their vacation.
The car had so much power!	Please draw a plane figure.	Did you squash that bug?	It was time to go to work.
That jacket is mine.	The litter was thrown away.	Grandma plays the organ on Sundays.	He had the lead in the school play.
Your bank account earns interest every month.	Will you please load the dryer for me?	I'll meet you at the theater at 8:00.	Where is the ground pepper?
She knocked on the door.	Are you a sports fan?	The baby has applesauce all over his face.	Which game would you like to play first?
He had a patch on the knee of his jeans.	You only need one application of shampoo to wash your hair.	Can you find the street on the map?	Did you flush the toilet?
Do you know how to pitch a tent?	You need to change your shoes.	The sign said, "Buy one, get one free."	You can form the line right here.
Start *	I like how you chose to accent the colors in your bedspread.	That's a sharp point on that pencil.	We need to pile into the van for the road trip.

Look at the boxes you did **not** highlight. Write the multiple-meaning word in each sentence.

1. ________ **4.** ________ **7.** ________ **10.** ________

2. ________ **5.** ________ **8.** ________ **11.** ________

3. ________ **6.** ________ **9.** ________ **12.** ________

Analogies

I have the **first card**.

Who has the rest of the analogy
old : elder : : young : ______

I have **love**.

Who has the rest of the analogy
trio : three : : duo : ______

I have **child**.

Who has the rest of the analogy
girl : twirl : : sound : ______

I have **two**.

Who has the rest of the analogy
water : waves : : snow : ______

I have **round**.

Who has the rest of the analogy
run : verb : : dog : ______

I have **drifts**.

Who has the rest of the analogy
success : achievement : : error : ______

I have **noun**.

Who has the rest of the analogy
smile : laugh : : tear : ______

I have **mistake**.

Who has the rest of the analogy
rose : flower : : pine : ______

I have **cry**.

Who has the rest of the analogy
detest : despise : : adore : ______

I have **tree**.

Who has the rest of the analogy
calf : cow : : lamb : ______

Analogies

I have **sheep**.

Who has the rest of the analogy
carpet : floor : : paint : ______

I have **wet**.

Who has the rest of the analogy
doctor : hospital : : teacher : ______

I have **wall**.

Who has the rest of the analogy
never : always : : none : ______

I have **school**.

Who has the rest of the analogy
car : drive : : oven: ______

I have **all**.

Who has the rest of the analogy
piano : key : : guitar : ______

I have **bake**.

Who has the rest of the analogy
frog : croak : : lion : ______

I have **string**.

Who has the rest of the analogy
digit : number : : letter : ______

I have **roar**.

Who has the rest of the analogy
sixth : fifth : : third : ______

I have **word**.

Who has the rest of the analogy
dark : light : : dry : ______

I have **second**.

Who has the rest of the analogy
swim : water : : ski : ______

Analogies

I have **snow**.

Who has the rest of the analogy
tile : mop : : carpet : ______

I have **skin**.

Who has the rest of the analogy
cold : milk : : hot : ______

I have **vacuum**.

Who has the rest of the analogy
school : learn : : bed : ______

I have **coffee**.

Who has the rest of the analogy
five : pentagon : : six : ______

I have **sleep**.

Who has the rest of the analogy
read : magazine : : listen : ______

I have **hexagon**.

Who has the rest of the analogy
sock : foot : : cap : ______

I have **radio**.

Who has the rest of the analogy
library : books : : bank : ______

I have **head**.

Who has the rest of the analogy
cowardly : brave : : selfish : ______

I have **money**.

Who has the rest of the analogy
podiatrist : feet : : dermatologist : ______

I have **generous**.

Who has the rest of the analogy
gaggle : geese : : swarm : ______

Analogies

I have **bees**.

Who has the rest of the analogy
horse : mare : : deer : ______

I have **paint**.

Who has the rest of the analogy
truck : garage : : airplane : ______

I have **doe**.

Who has the rest of the analogy
homerun : baseball : : touchdown : ______

I have **hangar**.

Who has the rest of the analogy
water : liquid : : ice : ______

I have **football**.

Who has the rest of the analogy
bowl : fish : : cage : ______

I have **solid**.

Who has the rest of the analogy
bird : parrot : : dog : ______

I have **hamster**.

Who has the rest of the analogy
a.m. : morning : : p.m. : ______

I have **poodle**.

Who has the rest of the analogy
sleep : bed : : work : ______

I have **evening**.

Who has the rest of the analogy
pencil : write : : brush : ______

I have **desk**.

Who has the first card?

Analogies

As your classmates identify the answers, highlight the letters that spell each word. Each new word is near the previous word. Words do not share letters and do not go backwards or diagonally. Clue: The first word is in the fourth row.

D	E	S	K	P	O	O	D	L	E	N	T	A	K	E
A	H	A	N	G	A	R	S	O	L	I	D	N	A	L
F	O	O	T	O	E	P	A	I	N	T	G	Y	I	S
C	H	I	L	D	V	H	F	A	C	B	E	E	S	G
O	M	P	A	R	E	A	O	D	O	E	R	C	H	E
C	R	Y	N	O	N	M	O	I	S	O	N	O	E	N
O	F	L	O	U	I	S	T	S	K	I	N	F	X	E
M	W	O	U	N	N	T	B	M	O	Y	R	F	A	R
I	D	V	N	D	G	E	A	O	R	O	S	E	G	O
S	T	E	T	W	O	R	L	N	A	U	H	E	O	U
T	D	R	I	F	T	S	L	E	D	N	A	T	N	S
A	A	A	L	L	S	R	E	Y	I	G	H	E	A	D
K	W	A	L	L	T	R	B	E	O	S	L	E	E	P
E	S	L	H	A	R	T	A	V	A	C	U	U	M	S
T	H	M	O	E	I	W	K	R	O	A	R	D	I	N
R	E	O	L	N	N	E	E	S	E	C	O	N	D	O
E	E	O	E	S	G	T	S	C	H	O	O	L	O	W
E	P	N	W	O	R	D	M	E	W	A	Y	T	R	Y

Solve the following analogies. Find the solutions in the word search above and highlight them.

1. hire : fire : : give : __ a __ __

2. look : see : : attempt : __ __ y

3. day : sun : : night : __ o __ __

4. hard : easy : : old : __ __ u __ __

5. hat : head : : sock : __ __ o t

6. bandage : cut : : patch : h __ __ __

HINT: If you did everything correctly, the remaining letters will spell a sentence.

A__ __

__ __.

Sentences—Declarative, Imperative, Interrogative, and Exclamatory

I have the **first card.**

Who has the declarative sentence about a carnival?

I have the sentence **My library books are five days overdue!**

Who has the declarative sentence about a cake?

I have the sentence **This carnival is fun.**

Who has the interrogative sentence about a pencil?

I have the sentence **My favorite dessert is chocolate cake.**

Who has the interrogative sentence about video games?

I have the sentence **May I borrow a pencil?**

Who has the exclamatory sentence about homework?

I have the sentence **Are you ready to play my new video game with me?**

Who has the declarative sentence about a dog?

I have the sentence **Oh no! I lost my homework!**

Who has the imperative sentence about rain?

I have the sentence **It's time to take my dog for a walk.**

Who has the imperative sentence about a garden?

I have the sentence **Put on your raincoat.**

Who has the exclamatory sentence about a library?

I have the sentence **Pick the tomatoes in the garden first.**

Who has the exclamatory sentence about soda?

Sentences—Declarative, Imperative, Interrogative, and Exclamatory

I have the sentence
My soda just spilled all over me!

Who has the imperative sentence about a cake?

I have the sentence
I'll use my new pencil.

Who has the interrogative sentence about homework?

I have the sentence
Don't lick the frosting before we cut the cake.

Who has the declarative sentence about rain?

I have the sentence
Where is your homework?

Who has the declarative sentence about a garden?

I have the sentence
It's raining hard today.

Who has the imperative sentence about a dog?

I have the sentence
I have roses in my garden.

Who has the exclamatory sentence about a carnival?

I have the sentence
Put the leash on your dog.

Who has the imperative sentence about a video game?

I have the sentence
What an exciting carnival ride!

Who has the imperative sentence about a library?

I have the sentence
Put that video game away right now.

Who has the declarative sentence about a pencil?

I have the sentence
Return that library book today.

Who has the declarative sentence about soda?

Sentences—Declarative, Imperative, Interrogative, and Exclamatory

I have the sentence
The bubbles in the soda upset my stomach.

Who has the interrogative sentence about a dog?

I have the sentence
Sharpen your pencil before class.

Who has the exclamatory sentence about a dog?

I have the sentence
Is that your golden retriever?

Who has the declarative sentence about a video game?

I have the sentence
That dog just bit me!

Who has the imperative sentence about a carnival?

I have the sentence
The video game is on that table.

Who has the interrogative sentence about a cake?

I have the sentence
Buy the tickets for the carnival.

Who has the exclamatory sentence about a garden?

I have the sentence
What kind of frosting would you like on the cake?

Who has the exclamatory sentence about rain?

I have the sentence
My garden is so beautiful!

Who has the declarative sentence about a library?

I have the sentence
Oh no! The rain caused a mudslide!

Who has the imperative sentence about a pencil?

I have the sentence
The library is closed.

Who has the interrogative sentence about rain?

Sentences—Declarative, Imperative, Interrogative, and Exclamatory

I have the sentence
Will this rain ever stop?

Who has the imperative sentence about a soda?

I have the sentence
Can we go to the carnival tomorrow?

Who has the imperative sentence about homework?

I have the sentence
Throw that soda can in the recycle bin.

Who has the interrogative sentence about a garden?

I have the sentence
Write your name on your homework.

Who has the exclamatory sentence about a cake?

I have the sentence
What kind of flowers did you plant in your garden?

Who has the exclamatory sentence about a video game?

I have the sentence
There's a fly on my birthday cake!

Who has the interrogative sentence about a library?

I have the sentence
My favorite video game is broken!

Who has the declarative sentence about homework?

I have the sentence
Where is the return bin for library books?

Who has the exclamatory sentence about a pencil?

I have the sentence
I turned in my homework on time.

Who has the interrogative sentence about a carnival?

I have the sentence
Ouch! His pencil poked me!

Who has the first card?

Sentences—Declarative, Imperative, Interrogative, and Exclamatory

Follow the path by highlighting the sentences as your classmates identify them.

MY FAVORITE VIDEO GAME IS BROKEN!	I TURNED IN MY HOMEWORK ON TIME.	**FINISH** * OUCH! HIS PENCIL POKED ME!	WHERE IS THE RETURN BIN FOR LIBRARY BOOKS?
WHAT KIND OF FLOWERS DID YOU PLANT IN YOUR GARDEN?	CAN WE GO TO THE CARNIVAL TOMORROW?	WRITE YOUR NAME ON YOUR HOMEWORK.	THERE'S A FLY ON MY BIRTHDAY CAKE!
THROW THAT SODA CAN IN THE RECYCLE BIN.	THE VIDEO GAME IS ON THAT TABLE.	IS THAT YOUR GOLDEN RETRIEVER?	THE BUBBLES IN THE SODA UPSET MY STOMACH.
WILL THIS RAIN EVER STOP?	WHAT KIND OF FROSTING WOULD YOU LIKE ON THE CAKE?	WHAT AN EXCITING CARNIVAL RIDE!	RETURN THAT LIBRARY BOOK TODAY.
THE LIBRARY IS CLOSED.	OH NO! THE RAIN CAUSED A MUDSLIDE!	I HAVE ROSES IN MY GARDEN.	SHE WENT TO THE PARK TO ENJOY A PICNIC.
MY GARDEN IS SO BEAUTIFUL!	SHARPEN YOUR PENCIL BEFORE CLASS.	WHERE IS YOUR HOMEWORK?	PUT THE PICNIC BASKET OVER THERE.
BUY THE TICKETS FOR THE CARNIVAL.	THAT DOG JUST BIT ME!	I'LL USE MY NEW PENCIL.	PUT THAT VIDEO GAME AWAY RIGHT NOW.
WHEN WILL WE LEAVE FOR THE PICNIC?	PICK THE TOMATOES IN THE GARDEN FIRST.	MY SODA JUST SPILLED ALL OVER ME!	PUT THE LEASH ON YOUR DOG.
THE ANTS ARE ALL OVER THE PICNIC BASKET!	IT'S TIME TO TAKE MY DOG FOR A WALK.	DON'T LICK THE FROSTING BEFORE WE CUT THE CAKE.	IT'S RAINING HARD TODAY.
MY FAVORITE DESSERT IS CHOCOLATE CAKE.	ARE YOU READY TO PLAY MY NEW VIDEO GAME WITH ME?	MAY I BORROW A PENCIL?	THIS CARNIVAL IS FUN.
MY LIBRARY BOOKS ARE FIVE DAYS OVERDUE!	PUT ON YOUR RAINCOAT.	OH NO! I LOST MY HOMEWORK!	**START** *

Look at the boxes you did **not** highlight. Write each sentence and label it as declarative, interrogative, imperative, or exclamatory.

1. ______________________________

2. ______________________________

3. ______________________________

4. ______________________________

Context Clues

I have the **first card**.

Who has the meaning of the word *exotic* in this sentence: Maria loves to cook *exotic* foods using spices from India.

I have **"convince."**

Who has the meaning of the word *browsing* in this sentence: They were *browsing* the book aisle of the store without planning to buy any books.

I have **"from other places."**

Who has the meaning of the word *extinguish* in this sentence: The firefighter tried to *extinguish* the flames.

I have **"looking at."**

Who has the meaning of the word *publications* in this sentence: This company produces many different *publications.*

I have **"put out."**

Who has the meaning of the word *fertile* in this sentence: The *fertile* soil helped her plants grow.

I have **"published works."**

Who has the meaning of the word *novel* in this sentence: It was such a *novel* idea to change a hanger into a flowerpot.

I have **"good for growing."**

Who has the meaning of the word *dramatic* in this sentence: The play was so *dramatic* that nobody smiled.

I have **"new and unusual."**

Who has the meaning of the word *match* in this sentence: She lost the tennis *match.*

I have **"serious."**

Who has the meaning of the word *persuade* in this sentence: She tried to *persuade* her mother into letting her stay up all night.

I have **"game."**

Who has the meaning of the word *disqualified* in this sentence: The player was *disqualified* for cheating in the game.

Context Clues

I have **"removed or kicked out."**

Who has the meaning of the word *elixir* in this sentence: The sick man felt better after drinking the *elixir*.

I have **"take apart."**

Who has the meaning of the word *endorse* in this sentence: Did you *endorse* the mayor in the last election?

I have **"medicine."**

Who has the meaning of the word *elated* in this sentence: The children were *elated* when they each received a present.

I have **"support."**

Who has the meaning of the word *obsolete* in this sentence: The use of the rotary dial telephone is almost *obsolete* now that we have cell phones.

I have **"excited."**

Who has the meaning of the word *alias* in this sentence: He used an *alias* to hide his real identity from the authorities.

I have **"out of use or out of fashion."**

Who has the meaning of the word *hoax* in this sentence: She played a sneaky *hoax* on her little brother.

I have **"fake name."**

Who has the meaning of the word *conceal* in this sentence: She found it difficult to *conceal* her true feelings.

I have **"trick."**

Who has the meaning of the word *wary* in this sentence: Paul is *wary* of spiders and always tries to avoid them.

I have **"hide."**

Who has the meaning of the word *dismantle* in this sentence: The mechanic needed to *dismantle* the engine before cleaning it.

I have **"cautious or watchful."**

Who has the meaning of the word *adjacent* in this sentence: The two friends live in *adjacent* houses so they spend a lot of time together.

Context Clues

I have **"next to or near."**

Who has the meaning of the word *gaped* in this sentence: The little boy *gaped* at the baby whale swimming for the first time in public.

I have **"flexible."**

Who has the meaning of the word *utter* in this sentence: The class didn't *utter* a word while the teacher stepped outside for a moment. They were so well behaved!

I have **"stared in amazement."**

Who has the meaning of the word *prevail* in this sentence: The captain felt that her team would improve and *prevail* in the next game.

I have **"speak."**

Who has the meaning of the word *obtain* in this sentence: The excited boy tried to *obtain* permission to go to his first sleepover.

I have **"win or be victorious."**

Who has the meaning of the word *zeal* in this sentence: Kim read the book with so much *zeal* that she finished it in one day.

I have **"get."**

Who has the meaning of the word *divulge* in this sentence: She promised to never *divulge* the secret.

I have **"enthusiasm."**

Who has the meaning of the word *stifle* in this sentence: Lara couldn't *stifle* her giggles as her brother tried to trick his friend, so she ruined the joke.

I have **"tell or reveal."**

Who has the meaning of the word *culprit* in this sentence: The *culprit* was caught with his hands in the "off limits" cookie jar.

I have **"hold back."**

Who has the meaning of the word *limber* in this sentence: Dancers are very *limber*, which explains how they can do so many twists and bends.

I have **"guilty person."**

Who has the meaning of the word *futile* in this sentence: It was *futile* to keep trying to open the lock, since the key broke off inside of it.

Context Clues

I have **"useless."**

Who has the meaning of the word *detests* in this sentence: The girl said that she *detests* yams. She refuses to eat them every time they are served.

I have **"shy."**

Who has the meaning of the word *fret* in this sentence: Try not to *fret* all night about your test tomorrow. You studied hard.

I have **"greatly dislikes."**

Who has the meaning of the word *expedite* in this sentence: She wanted to *expedite* her Internet order, so she paid for overnight delivery.

I have **"worry."**

Who has the meaning of the word *dispute* in this sentence: The players got into a *dispute* over whether the ball made it into the basket before the buzzer.

I have **"speed up."**

Who has the meaning of the word *income* in this sentence: She is trying to save as much of her *income* as she can to pay for her son's college.

I have **"argument or disagreement."**

Who has the meaning of the word *toxic* in this sentence: The *toxic* liquids were kept out of the reach of the children.

I have **"money earned."**

Who has the meaning of the word *collapse* in this sentence: The runner thought he would *collapse* at the end of the exhausting marathon.

I have **"poisonous."**

Who has the meaning of the word *trek* in this sentence: She felt like the hike was the longest *trek* she had ever taken.

I have **"fall down due to a loss of strength."**

Who has the meaning of the word *timid* in this sentence: The boy was so *timid* that he hardly ever talked to people.

I have **"journey."**

Who has the first card?

Context Clues

Follow the path by highlighting the answers as your classmates identify them.

FERTILE	ARGUMENT OR DISAGREEMENT	WORRY	SHY	PERSUADE
FINISH * JOURNEY	POISONOUS	MONEY EARNED	FALL DOWN DUE TO A LOSS OF STRENGTH	PUBLICATIONS
DISQUALIFIED	CONCEAL	SPEED UP	GUILTY PERSON	TELL OR REVEAL
FROM OTHER PLACES	PUT OUT	GREATLY DISLIKES	USELESS	GET
START *	GOOD FOR GROWING	SUPPORT	OUT OF USE OR OUT OF FASHION	SPEAK
HOAX	SERIOUS	TAKE APART	TRICK	FLEXIBLE
LOOKING AT	CONVINCE	HIDE	CAUTIOUS OR WATCHFUL	HOLD BACK
PUBLISHED WORKS	OBTAIN	FAKE NAME	NEXT TO OR NEAR	ENTHUSIASM
NEW AND UNUSUAL	GAME	EXCITED	STARED IN AMAZEMENT	WIN OR BE VICTORIOUS
CULPRIT	REMOVED OR KICKED OUT	MEDICINE	INCOME	TOXIC

Look at the boxes you did **not** highlight. The words left over were used in the game. Write a sentence for each word.

1. ____________________

2. ____________________

3. ____________________

4. ____________________

5. ____________________

6. ____________________

7. ____________________

8. ____________________

9. ____________________

10. ____________________

Main Idea and Details 1

I have the **first card**.

Who has the main idea for these details: banjo, flute, and organ.

I have **fruits**.

Who has the main idea for these details: magenta, teal, and navy.

I have **musical instruments**.

Who has the main idea for these details: trout, herring, and tuna.

I have **colors**.

Who has the main idea for these details: garter, viper, and boa constrictor.

I have **fish**.

Who has the main idea for these details: mouse, monitor, and keyboard.

I have **snakes**.

Who has the main idea for these details: pentagon, trapezoid, and square.

I have **computers**.

Who has the main idea for these details: bear, whale, and raccoon.

I have **shapes**.

Who has the main idea for these details: tulip, rose, and daffodil.

I have **mammals**.

Who has the main idea for these details: bananas, oranges, and lemons.

I have **flowers**.

Who has the main idea for these details: falcon, eagle, and hawk.

Main Idea and Details 1

I have **birds**.

Who has the main idea for these details: teak, oak, and pine.

I have **coins**.

Who has the main idea for these details: milk, water, and juice.

I have **trees**.

Who has the main idea for these details: treadmill, weights, and bike.

I have **things you drink**.

Who has the main idea for these details: lungs, heart, and liver.

I have **exercise equipment**.

Who has the main idea for these details: hat, cap, and headband.

I have **organs**.

Who has the main idea for these details: bee, wasp, and yellow jacket.

I have **things you wear on your head**.

Who has the main idea for these details: chess, checkers, and backgammon.

I have **insects**.

Who has the main idea for these details: dens, caves, and burrows.

I have **board games**.

Who has the main idea for these details: pennies, quarters, and dimes.

I have **animal homes**.

Who has the main idea for these details: owl, deer, and skunk.

Main Idea and Details 1

I have **forest animals**.

Who has the main idea for these details: silk, honey, and milk.

I have **things you read**.

Who has the main idea for these details: history, math, and science.

I have **things we get from animals**.

Who has the main idea for these details: chicken, pig, and goat.

I have **school subjects**.

Who has the main idea for these details: pond, lake, and river.

I have **farm animals**.

Who has the main idea for these details: turnip, carrot, and broccoli.

I have **bodies of water**.

Who has the main idea for these details: pan, pot, and skillet.

I have **vegetables**.

Who has the main idea for these details: clouds, moon, and sun.

I have **things you use to cook**.

Who has the main idea for these details: happy, sad, and angry.

I have **things in the sky**.

Who has the main idea for these details: magazine, book, and newspaper.

I have **emotions**.

Who has the main idea for these details: socks, shoes, and slippers.

Main Idea and Details 1

I have **things you wear on your feet**.

Who has the main idea for these details: pretzels, chips, and popcorn.

I have **snacks**.

Who has the main idea for these details: chocolate, raspberry, and vanilla.

I have **flavors**.

Who has the main idea for these details: hop, run, and walk.

I have **ways to move**.

Who has the main idea for these details: canoe, kayak, and ship.

I have **water transportation vehicles**.

Who has the main idea for these details: tent, lantern, and sleeping bag.

I have **camping gear**.

Who has the main idea for these details: title page, table of contents, and index.

I have **parts of a book**.

Who has the main idea for these details: tape, glue, and rubber band.

I have **things that hold items together**.

Who has the main idea for these details: cake, presents, and games.

I have **things at a birthday party**.

Who has the main idea for these details: bottle, rattle, and diapers.

I have **things for a baby**.

Who has the first card?

I Have, Who Has?: Language Arts • 3–4 © 2006 Creative Teaching Press

Main Idea and Details 1

Follow the path by highlighting the answers as your classmates identify them.

START*	MUSICAL INSTRUMENTS	THINGS THAT ARE BLUE	COLORS
REPTILES	FISH	FRUITS	SNAKES
BOARD GAMES	COMPUTERS	MAMMALS	SHAPES
COINS	THINGS YOU WEAR ON YOUR HEAD	AMPHIBIANS	FLOWERS
THINGS YOU DRINK	EXERCISE EQUIPMENT	TREES	BIRDS
ORGANS	FOREST ANIMALS	THINGS WE GET FROM ANIMALS	FARM ANIMALS
INSECTS	ANIMAL HOMES	AUTOMOBILES	VEGETABLES
EMOTIONS	THINGS YOU USE TO COOK	THINGS YOU READ	THINGS IN THE SKY
THINGS YOU WEAR ON YOUR FEET	BODIES OF WATER	SCHOOL SUBJECTS	WATER TRANSPORTATION VEHICLES
SNACKS	FLAVORS	WAYS TO MOVE	CAMPING GEAR
THINGS FOR A BABY **FINISH ***	THINGS AT A BIRTHDAY PARTY	THINGS THAT HOLD ITEMS TOGETHER	PARTS OF A BOOK

Identify the main idea for each set of details.

1. pugs, poodles, labs, Chihuahuas ____ ____ e e ____ ____ of ____ ____ g ____

2. soda, water, juice, milk b e ____ e r a ____ e ____

3. motor, brakes, door, tires p ____ r ____ s of a ____ a ____

4. gouda, cheddar, mozzarella, swiss c ____ e ____ ____ ____ s

5. rye, pumpernickel, wheat, white b ____ ____ a ____ s

6. chrysalis, metamorphosis, caterpillar, beautiful ____ u ____ ____ ____ r ____ ____ y

Main Idea and Details 2

I have the **first card**.

Who has a detail to support the main idea "colors"?

I have **sandcastles**.

Who has a detail to support the main idea "hobbies"?

I have **yellow**.

Who has a detail to support the main idea "sources of light"?

I have **building model cars**.

Who has a detail to support the main idea "cameras"?

I have **nightlight**.

Who has a detail to support the main idea "types of books"?

I have **focus**.

Who has a detail to support the main idea "diseases"?

I have **realistic fiction**.

Who has a detail to support the main idea "circus"?

I have **chicken pox**.

Who has a detail to support the main idea "yellow things"?

I have **lions**.

Who has a detail to support the main idea "beach"?

I have **bananas**.

Who has a detail to support the main idea "dogs"?

Main Idea and Details 2

I have **terriers**.

Who has a detail to support the main idea "basic shapes"?

I have **lines**.

Who has a detail to support the main idea "appliances in a kitchen"?

I have **triangle**.

Who has a detail to support the main idea "words that rhyme with *dice*"?

I have **dishwasher**.

Who has a detail to support the main idea "meats"?

I have **device**.

Who has a detail to support the main idea "things on a calendar"?

I have **roast beef**.

Who has a detail to support the main idea "things you can roast"?

I have **months**.

Who has a detail to support the main idea "jewelry"?

I have **marshmallows**.

Who has a detail to support the main idea "hot drinks"?

I have **earrings**.

Who has a detail to support the main idea "things on a road"?

I have **hot chocolate**.

Who has a detail to support the main idea "hamburger"?

Main Idea and Details 2

I have **ketchup**. Who has a detail to support the main idea "days of the week"?	I have **channel**. Who has a detail to support the main idea "breads"?
I have **Friday**. Who has a detail to support the main idea "relatives"?	I have **rye**. Who has a detail to support the main idea "sports"?
I have **grandma**. Who has a detail to support the main idea "parts of a bird"?	I have **basketball**. Who has a detail to support the main idea "parts of the mouth"?
I have **beak**. Who has a detail to support the main idea "ice cream sundae"?	I have **tongue**. Who has a detail to support the main idea "senses"?
I have **ice cream**. Who has a detail to support the main idea "television"?	I have **sight**. Who has a detail to support the main idea "restaurant"?

Main Idea and Details 2

I have **waiters**.

Who has a detail to support the main idea "tools"?

I have **transmission**.

Who has a detail to support the main idea "things in a frame"?

I have **saw**.

Who has a detail to support the main idea "weather conditions"?

I have **photos**.

Who has a detail to support the main idea "desserts"?

I have **foggy**.

Who has a detail to support the main idea "school jobs"?

I have **brownies**.

Who has a detail to support the main idea "dog items"?

I have **custodian**.

Who has a detail to support the main idea "building materials"?

I have **leash**.

Who has a detail to support the main idea "red things"?

I have **plaster**.

Who has a detail to support the main idea "parts of a car"?

I have **wagon**.

Who has the first card?

Main Idea and Details 2

Fill in the missing letters of the words as your classmates identify the answers. Start at the arrow and go from left to right and top to bottom.

START →	_ E _ _ _ W	_ I _ _ _ _ I _ H _	R _ _ _ I S _ I _ F _ _ T _ _ N
_ _ O _ _	_ A _ _ C _ S T _ _ _	_ U I _ _ _ _ _ _ O _ E _ _ A _ _	_ O C _ _
_ _ I _ _ E _ _ _ X	_ _ N A _ _ S	_ E _ R I E _ S	_ _ I _ _ G _ _
_ _ V _ C _	_ O _ _ _ _	E A _ R _ _ _ _	_ _ _ E _
_ I _ _ _ A _ _ _ _	_ _ A _ _ _ _ _ _	M _ _ S H M _ _ _ _ _ S	H _ _ C H _ _ O _ A T E
K E T _ _ _ _	_ _ _ _ _ Y	_ _ A _ _ _ _	_ E A _
_ _ _ _ _ E A _	_ _ A _ _ E _	_ Y E	_ A _ _ _ _ _ _ _ _ _
_ O _ G U E	_ _ G H _	_ A I _ _ _ _	_ _ W
_ O _ _ _	_ U _ _ _ _ I A _	_ _ A _ _ _ _	_ _ A _ _ _ I _ _ _ _ _
_ _ O _ _ _	_ _ O W _ I _ _	_ E A _ _	_ A _ O _
A	B	C	D

List the words in Column C. Write at least two more details that could join each word to create a main idea. Write a main idea.

1. ____________ with ____________ and ____________ fit into the main idea ________________.
2. ____________ with ____________ and ____________ fit into the main idea ________________.
3. ____________ with ____________ and ____________ fit into the main idea ________________.
4. ____________ with ____________ and ____________ fit into the main idea ________________.
5. ____________ with ____________ and ____________ fit into the main idea ________________.
6. ____________ with ____________ and ____________ fit into the main idea ________________.
7. ____________ with ____________ and ____________ fit into the main idea ________________.
8. ____________ with ____________ and ____________ fit into the main idea ________________.
9. ____________ with ____________ and ____________ fit into the main idea ________________.
10. ____________ with ____________ and ____________ fit into the main idea ________________.

Categorization

I have the **first card**.

Who has the word that doesn't belong in the same category as the other words: circle, rectangle, number, diamond.

I have **circle**.

Who has the word that doesn't belong in the same category as the other words: nose, mouth, foot, eye.

I have **number**.

Who has the word that doesn't belong in the same category as the other words: pond, lake, country, river.

I have **foot**.

Who has the word that doesn't belong in the same category as the other words: quartz, limestone, quarter, granite.

I have **country**.

Who has the word that doesn't belong in the same category as the other words: carnation, petunia, violet, sycamore.

I have **quarter**.

Who has the word that doesn't belong in the same category as the other words: glue, paste, granite, tape.

I have **sycamore**.

Who has the word that doesn't belong in the same category as the other words: morning, penny, afternoon, night.

I have **granite**.

Who has the word that doesn't belong in the same category as the other words: alligator, river, python, cobra.

I have **penny**.

Who has the word that doesn't belong in the same category as the other words: square, rectangle, parallelogram, circle.

I have **river**.
Who has the word that doesn't belong in the same category as the other words: north, south, map, west.

Categorization

I have **map**.

Who has the word that doesn't belong in the same category as the other words: pants, shirt, umbrella, jacket.

I have **Los Angeles**.

Who has the word that doesn't belong in the same category as the other words: beret, pants, cap, bonnet.

I have **umbrella**.

Who has the word that doesn't belong in the same category as the other words: pink, green, orange, carnation.

I have **pants**.

Who has the word that doesn't belong in the same category as the other words: south, prairie, tundra, desert.

I have **carnation**.

Who has the word that doesn't belong in the same category as the other words: butterfly, ladybug, alligator, moth.

I have **south**.

Who has the word that doesn't belong in the same category as the other words: Hawaii, Africa, Australia, Europe.

I have **alligator**.

Who has the word that doesn't belong in the same category as the other words: nose, hands, feet, eyes.

I have **Hawaii**.

Who has the word that doesn't belong in the same category as the other words: peas, orange, lettuce, asparagus.

I have **nose**.

Who has the word that doesn't belong in the same category as the other words: Texas, Los Angeles, Hawaii, Utah.

I have **orange**.

Who has the word that doesn't belong in the same category as the other words: yard, week, month, year.

Categorization

I have **yard**.

Who has the word that doesn't belong in the same category as the other words: stem, leaf, root, soil.

I have **year**.

Who has the word that doesn't belong in the same category as the other words: leaf, coffee, milk, tea.

I have **soil**.

Who has the word that doesn't belong in the same category as the other words: violin, harp, cello, tango.

I have **leaf**.

Who has the word that doesn't belong in the same category as the other words: violin, mambo, salsa, ballet.

I have **tango**.

Who has the word that doesn't belong in the same category as the other words: tornado, cyclone, motorcycle, hurricane.

I have **violin**.

Who has the word that doesn't belong in the same category as the other words: dribble, run, jump, skip.

I have **motorcycle**.

Who has the word that doesn't belong in the same category as the other words: dribble, hoop, rebound, goalie.

I have **dribble**.

Who has the word that doesn't belong in the same category as the other words: rain, snow, tornado, hail.

I have **goalie**.

Who has the word that doesn't belong in the same category as the other words: seconds, minutes, hours, year.

I have **tornado**.

Who has the word that doesn't belong in the same category as the other words: cake, pie, cookie, pizza.

Categorization

I have **pizza**.

Who has the word that doesn't belong in the same category as the other words: sand, water, waves, snow.

I have **sand**.

Who has the word that doesn't belong in the same category as the other words: salami, cookie, bologna, ham.

I have **snow**.

Who has the word that doesn't belong in the same category as the other words: election, ballet, president, vote.

I have **cookie**.

Who has the word that doesn't belong in the same category as the other words: computer, mouse, glossary, keyboard.

I have **ballet**.

Who has the word that doesn't belong in the same category as the other words: index, glossary, encyclopedia, preface.

I have **glossary**.

Who has the word that doesn't belong in the same category as the other words: bake, milk, broil, boil.

I have **encyclopedia**.

Who has the word that doesn't belong in the same category as the other words: happy, angry, election, frustrated.

I have **milk**.

Who has the word that doesn't belong in the same category as the other words: parrot, mouse, cardinal, bluejay.

I have **election**.

Who has the word that doesn't belong in the same category as the other words: sand, shoe, sandal, boot.

I have **mouse**.

Who has the first card?

Categorization

Follow the path by highlighting the words as your classmates identify them.

HORSE	START *	NUMBER
PENNY	SYCAMORE	COUNTRY
CIRCLE	GRANITE	RIVER
FOOT	QUARTER	MAP
LOS ANGELES	NOSE	UMBRELLA
PANTS	ALLIGATOR	CARNATION
SOUTH	HAWAII	PIANO
YARD	ORANGE	PURPLE
SOIL	GOALIE	YEAR
TANGO	MOTORCYCLE	LEAF
SNOW	PIZZA	VIOLIN
BALLET	TORNADO	DRIBBLE
ENCYCLOPEDIA	COOKIE	GLOSSARY
ELECTION	SAND	MILK
BANANA	FINISH *	MOUSE

Look at the boxes you did **not** highlight. Write each word. Then write two other words that would fit in the same category as the word.

1. ______________________ ______________________ ______________________

2. ______________________ ______________________ ______________________

3. ______________________ ______________________ ______________________

4. ______________________ ______________________ ______________________

Fact or Opinion?

I have the **first card**.

Who has a fact about ice cream?

I have the sentence **Math is the most difficult subject.**

Who has a fact about bees?

I have the sentence **Ice cream is a dairy product.**

Who has a fact about rainbows?

I have the sentence **Bees produce honey.**

Who has an opinion about soccer?

I have the sentence **Rainbows are often visible after a rainstorm.**

Who has an opinion about football?

I have the sentence **My team will win the next soccer game.**

Who has a fact about water skiing?

I have the sentence **All the football players do is tackle each other.**

Who has a fact about a city?

I have the sentence **A person needs a boat to water ski.**

Who has an opinion about school?

I have the sentence **A city is usually run by a mayor.**

Who has an opinion about math?

I have the sentence **We go to the best school in our state.**

Who has a fact about snakes?

Fact or Opinion?

I have the sentence
Snakes are members of the reptile family.

Who has an opinion about homework?

I have the sentence
A person can never have too many fish in an aquarium.

Who has a fact about bats?

I have the sentence
Our teacher assigns too much homework.

Who has a fact about turtles?

I have the sentence
Bats are nocturnal animals.

Who has a fact about sewing?

I have the sentence
Turtles move very slowly.

Who has an opinion about the rain forest?

I have the sentence
Needles are used to sew.

Who has an opinion about water?

I have the sentence
The rain forest is the safest place to vacation.

Who has a fact about hamsters?

I have the sentence
Drinking bottled water is better for your body.

Who has a fact about math?

I have the sentence
Hamsters use an exercise wheel.

Who has an opinion about fish?

I have the sentence
Multiplication is a skill learned in math.

Who has an opinion about snakes?

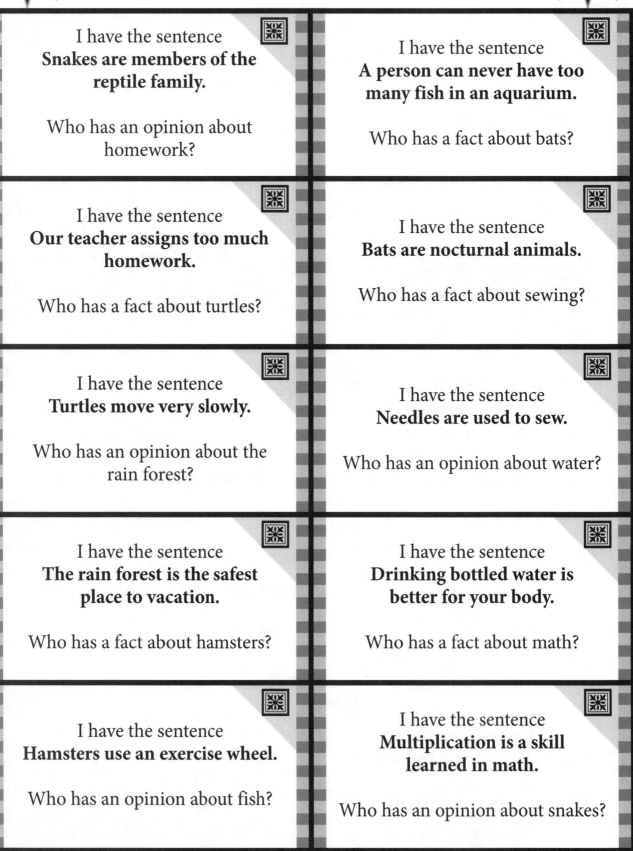

Fact or Opinion?

I have the sentence
Snakes are creepy and slimy.

Who has an opinion about bubble gum?

I have the sentence
Ice cream is best between two cookies.

Who has an opinion about hamsters?

I have the sentence
Every child loves chewing bubble gum.

Who has a fact about homework?

I have the sentence
Hamsters are cute and cuddly.

Who has a fact about school?

I have the sentence
The purpose of homework is to help you practice and learn.

Who has a fact about water?

I have the sentence
Children and adults can attend school.

Who has a fact about soccer?

I have the sentence
It is unsafe to drink ocean water.

Who has a fact about cruise ships?

I have the sentence
The team with the most goals in a soccer game wins.

Who has an opinion about bees?

I have the sentence
Cruise ships carry people on vacations all over the world.

Who has an opinion about ice cream?

I have the sentence
Bees are angry insects.

Who has an opinion about cruise ships?

Fact or Opinion?

I have the sentence
Vacations on cruise ships are the most luxurious.

Who has a fact about bubble gum?

I have the sentence
Turtles look very old.

Who has an opinion about the city?

I have the sentence
Many schools do not allow bubble gum chewing on campus.

Who has an opinion about sewing?

I have the sentence
The city is too crowded.

Who has an opinion about bats?

I have the sentence
Every parent should know how to sew.

Who has a fact about the rain forest?

I have the sentence
Bats are scary.

Who has an opinion about skiing?

I have the sentence
Many species in the rain forest are endangered.

Who has a fact about football?

I have the sentence
Children under the age of sixteen shouldn't be allowed to ski.

Who has an opinion about rainbows?

I have the sentence
A touchdown scores six points in football.

Who has an opinion about turtles?

I have the sentence
Rainbows are more beautiful than sunsets.

Who has the first card?

Fact or Opinion?

Follow the path by highlighting the facts and opinions as your classmates identify them.

CHILDREN UNDER THE AGE OF SIXTEEN SHOULDN'T BE ALLOWED TO SKI.	**FINISH** * RAINBOWS ARE MORE BEAUTIFUL THAN SUNSETS.	THE INTERNET IS AVAILABLE AROUND THE WORLD.
BATS ARE SCARY.	EVERY PARENT SHOULD KNOW HOW TO SEW.	MANY SCHOOLS DO NOT ALLOW BUBBLE GUM CHEWING ON CAMPUS.
THE CITY IS TOO CROWDED.	MANY SPECIES IN THE RAINFOREST ARE ENDANGERED.	VACATIONS ON CRUISE SHIPS ARE THE MOST LUXURIOUS.
TURTLES LOOK VERY OLD.	A TOUCHDOWN SCORES SIX POINTS IN FOOTBALL.	BEES ARE ANGRY INSECTS.
THAT SHOW IS THE BEST!	YOU SHOULD PLAY ON THE BASEBALL TEAM.	THE TEAM WITH THE MOST GOALS IN THE SOCCER GAME WINS.
EVERY CHILD LOVES TO EAT PIZZA.	MANY TEENAGERS HAVE CELL PHONES.	CHILDREN AND ADULTS CAN ATTEND SCHOOL.
DRINKING BOTTLED WATER IS BETTER FOR YOUR BODY.	MULTIPLICATION IS A SKILL LEARNED IN MATH.	HAMSTERS ARE CUTE AND CUDDLY.
NEEDLES ARE USED TO SEW.	SNAKES ARE CREEPY AND SLIMY.	ICE CREAM IS BEST BETWEEN TWO COOKIES.
BATS ARE NOCTURNAL ANIMALS.	EVERY CHILD LOVES CHEWING BUBBLE GUM.	CRUISE SHIPS CARRY PEOPLE ON VACATIONS ALL OVER THE WORLD.
A PERSON CAN NEVER HAVE TOO MANY FISH IN AN AQUARIUM.	THE PURPOSE OF HOMEWORK IS TO HELP YOU PRACTICE AND LEARN.	IT IS UNSAFE TO DRINK OCEAN WATER.
HAMSTERS USE AN EXERCISE WHEEL.	MY TEAM WILL WIN THE NEXT SOCCER GAME.	BEES PRODUCE HONEY.
THE RAINFOREST IS THE SAFEST PLACE TO VACATION.	A PERSON NEEDS A BOAT TO WATER SKI.	MATH IS THE MOST DIFFICULT SUBJECT.
TURTLES MOVE VERY SLOWLY.	WE GO TO THE BEST SCHOOL IN OUR STATE.	A CITY IS USUALLY RUN BY A MAYOR.
OUR TEACHER ASSIGNS TOO MUCH HOMEWORK.	SNAKES ARE MEMBERS OF THE REPTILE FAMILY.	ALL THE FOOTBALL PLAYERS DO IS TACKLE EACH OTHER.
START *	ICE CREAM IS A DAIRY PRODUCT.	RAINBOWS ARE OFTEN VISIBLE AFTER A RAINSTORM.

Look at the boxes you did **not** highlight. Write the sentences. Identify each sentence as a fact or an opinion.

1. ______________________________

2. ______________________________

3. ______________________________

4. ______________________________

5. ______________________________

Vocabulary 1

I have the **first card**.

Who has the word that means "shocked or surprised"?

I have **schedule**.

Who has the word that means "created in a unique way"?

I have **astonished**.

Who has the word that means "to keep doing something"?

I have **invented**.

Who has the word that means "looked for ways things were the same"?

I have **continue**.

Who has the word that means "common"?

I have **compared**.

Who has the word that means "looked for ways things were different"?

I have **ordinary**.

Who has the word that means "a protective place to live"?

I have **contrasted**.

Who has the word that means "interested in learning"?

I have **shelter**.

Who has the word that means "a plan with a time table"?

I have **curious**.

Who has the word that means "fell down in a clumsy way"?

Vocabulary 1

I have **stumbled**.

Who has the word that means "told someone to keep trying"?

I have **whirling**.

Who has the word that means "friendly with people"?

I have **encouraged**.

Who has the word that means "mistake"?

I have **social**.

Who has the word that means "slowly"?

I have **error**.

Who has the word that means "disappeared"?

I have **gradually**.

Who has the word that means "pictures in a book"?

I have **vanished**.

Who has the word that means "a sealed container"?

I have **illustrations**.

Who has the word that means "the words under pictures in a book"?

I have **canister**.

Who has the word that means "spinning around"?

I have **captions**.

Who has the word that means "said in a proud way"?

Vocabulary 1

I have **proclaimed**.

Who has the word that means "difficulties"?

I have **climate**.

Who has the word that means "passed around"?

I have **hardships**.

Who has the word that means "to think"?

I have **circulated**.

Who has the word that means "people on the opposite team"?

I have **ponder**.

Who has the word that means "moved quickly"?

I have **opponents**.

Who has the word that means "enemy"?

I have **darted**.

Who has the word that means "a bad feeling about doing something wrong"?

I have **foe**.

Who has the word that means "relatives of long ago"?

I have **guilt**.

Who has the word that means "the weather conditions"?

I have **ancestors**.

Who has the word that means "worried about something"?

Vocabulary 1

I have **fretted**.

Who has the word that means "information you have learned"?

I have **eldest**.

Who has the word that means "you allowed someone to enter"?

I have **knowledge**.

Who has the word that means "things you have to do"?

I have **admitted**.

Who has the word that means "looking at carefully"?

I have **errands**.

Who has the word that means to "draw quickly, usually with a pencil"?

I have **inspecting**.

Who has the word that means "set free"?

I have **sketch**.

Who has the word that means "established" or "set up"?

I have **released**.

Who has the word that means "very sad, usually related to grief"?

I have **founded**.

Who has the word that means "the oldest person"?

I have **tragic**.

Who has the first card?

Vocabulary 1

Fill in the missing letters of the words as your classmates identify the answers. Start at the arrow and go from left to right and top to bottom.

START →	A _ _ O _ I _ _ _ _	_ _ _ _ _ _ _ U E	_ _ _ I _ A _ Y
_ _ E _ _ _ _	_ C H E _ U _ _	_ _ _ E _ _ _ _	_ O M _ _ _ _ _ _
_ _ _ _ R A _ _ _ _	_ U _ I O U _	_ _ U M _ _ _ _	E _ _ O U R A _ E _
E _ _ O _	_ A _ I _ _ E _	_ A _ _ _ T _ _	W H I _ _ _ _ _ _
_ _ C I A _	_ _ _ _ U A _ _ _	I _ _ U _ _ _ A T _ _ _ _	_ A _ T _ _ _ _
_ _ _ _ _ _ A I M _ _	_ _ _ _ _ _ _ _ I _ S	_ O _ _ E _	_ A _ _ _ _ _
_ U I _ _	_ _ I _ A _ E	C I _ C U _ _ _ _ _ _	O _ _ O N E N _ _
_ _ E	_ _ C E _ _ O _ _	F _ _ T T _ _	K N _ W _ E D G _
E _ _ A _ _ _	_ K _ T _ _	_ O U _ _ _ _	E _ _ E _ _
A _ _ _ T T _ _	I _ _ _ E _ _ _ _ _ _	_ _ _ E A _ _ _	_ _ A G _ _
A	**B**	**C**	**D**

Use each word from Column C in a sentence.

1. ______________________________
2. ______________________________
3. ______________________________
4. ______________________________
5. ______________________________
6. ______________________________
7. ______________________________
8. ______________________________
9. ______________________________
10. ______________________________

Vocabulary 2

I have the **first card**.

Who has the word that means "to put into service"?

I have **audition**.

Who has the word that means "half asleep"?

I have **utilize**.

Who has the word that means "to urge or talk someone into something"?

I have **drowsy**.

Who has the word that means "to grab or take hold of something"?

I have **coax**.

Who has the word that means "a quick reflex response to sudden pain"?

I have **seize**.

Who has the word that means "to move toward something"?

I have **flinch**.

Who has the word that means "an overwhelming feeling of fear"?

I have **approach**.

Who has the word that means "causing much damage"?

I have **terror**.

Who has the word that means "to perform in order to get a role in a play, musical, or show"?

I have **destructive**.

Who has the word that means "fully developed"?

Vocabulary 2

I have **mature**.

Who has the word that means "to ask to do something"?

I have **detest**.

Who has the word that means "the inside region or area of something"?

I have **request**.

Who has the word that means "to try something"?

I have **interior**.

Who has the word that means "to refuse to do something"?

I have **attempt**.

Who has the word that means "to predict how something will develop"?

I have **resist**.

Who has the word that means "happening every year"?

I have **forecast**.

Who has the word that means "very special and of high worth or cost"?

I have **annual**.

Who has the word that means "feelings of jealousy"?

I have **precious**.

Who has the word that means "to dislike intensely"?

I have **envy**.

Who has the word that means "the person who tells a story"?

Vocabulary 2

I have **narrator**.

Who has the word that means "surprised and unplanned"?

I have **cardigan**.

Who has the word that means "fun things to do"?

I have **unexpected**.

Who has the word that means "upset with feelings of a lack of control"?

I have **entertainment**.

Who has the word that means "on time"?

I have **frustrated**.

Who has the word that means "movement"?

I have **prompt**.

Who has the word that means "evenly spaced periods of time"?

I have **motion**.

Who has the word that means "the feel of something"?

I have **intervals**.

Who has the word that means "tiny in size"?

I have **texture**.

Who has the word that means "a long-sleeved sweater that buttons up the front"?

I have **petite**.

Who has the word that describes "something with a smell"?

Vocabulary 2

I have **scented**.

Who has the word that describes "something that cannont be ruined"?

I have **temporary**.

Who has the word that means "common"?

I have **indestructible**.

Who has the word that means "power"?

I have **ordinary**.

Who has the word that means "few of something are available"?

I have **strength**.

Who has the word that means "leaning back"?

I have **scarce**.

Who has the word that means "to go down"?

I have **reclining**.

Who has the word that describes "something that does not have a scent"?

I have **descend**.

Who has the word that means "careful"?

I have **odorless**.

Who has the word that describes "something that can be changed at any time"?

I have **cautious**.

Who has the first card?

Vocabulary 2

As your classmates identify the answers, highlight the letters that spell each word. Each new word is near the previous word. Words do not share letters and do not go backwards or diagonally. Clue: The first word is in the fourth column.

T	E	M	P	O	R	A	R	Y	O	D	O	R	L	E	S	S	A	A
O	R	E	C	L	I	N	I	N	G	A	E	I	O	U	C	A	U	U
R	S	T	R	E	N	G	T	H	I	N	F	O	R	M	A	F	T	D
D	I	N	D	E	S	T	R	U	C	T	I	B	L	E	R	R	H	I
I	S	E	N	T	E	R	T	A	I	N	M	E	N	T	D	U	E	T
N	C	P	U	C	O	A	X	F	A	E	I	O	U	I	I	S	N	I
A	E	R	T	I	I	O	T	L	A	E	E	A	I	O	G	T	T	O
R	N	O	I	U	A	A	E	I	P	R	O	F	I	T	A	R	I	N
Y	T	M	L	S	D	U	R	N	U	U	O	I	A	E	N	A	C	E
S	E	P	I	E	R	D	R	C	T	E	X	T	U	R	E	T	U	I
C	D	T	Z	I	O	I	O	H	A	M	O	T	I	O	N	E	A	U
A	P	I	E	Z	W	T	R	P	E	N	A	L	T	Y	O	D	N	U
R	E	N	A	E	S	I	U	N	E	X	P	E	C	T	E	D	N	I
C	T	T	P	A	Y	O	E	I	N	A	R	R	A	T	O	R	U	N
E	I	E	P	A	E	N	I	O	U	U	A	I	E	N	V	Y	A	T
D	T	R	R	D	E	S	T	R	U	C	T	I	V	E	I	U	L	E
E	E	V	O	M	A	T	U	R	E	U	A	R	E	S	I	S	T	R
S	A	A	A	A	R	E	Q	U	E	S	T	O	A	E	I	O	U	I
C	I	L	C	I	O	A	T	T	E	M	P	T	O	U	I	E	A	O
E	O	S	H	F	O	R	E	C	A	S	T	E	I	O	U	U	E	R
N	U	U	A	O	P	R	E	C	I	O	U	S	D	E	T	E	S	T
D	C	A	U	T	I	O	U	S	O	A	F	L	E	X	I	B	L	E

Look at the letters you did **not** highlight. Locate the following vocabulary words in the word search. Then use each word in a sentence. Write your sentences on the back of this paper. Use a dictionary, if needed.

1. flexible
2. authentic
3. audition
4. profit
5. inform
6. penalty

HINT: If you did everything correctly, all the remaining letters are vowels.

Vocabulary in Context 1

I have the **first card**.

Who has the missing word in this sentence: Everyone sat in the ____ to watch the air show.

I have **disappointed**.

Who has the missing word in this sentence: He felt so ____ of himself when he shot the winning basket.

I have **meadow**.

Who has the missing word in this sentence: There was a clear ____ through the forest.

I have **proud**.

Who has the missing word in this sentence: Maria felt it was ____ for her older sister to get a bigger allowance than her.

I have **passage**.

Who has the missing word in this sentence: Lisa was ____ that someone took her favorite pencil.

I have **unfair**.

Who has the missing word in this sentence: Devon was so ____ that he ate every cookie without even sharing a crumb.

I have **furious**.

Who has the missing word in this sentence: Roy tried to ____ the total cost.

I have **greedy**.

Who has the missing word in this sentence: Sari loved hearing ____ about how smart she was in math.

I have **calculate**.

Who has the missing word in this sentence: She was ____ when her grade was lower than she expected.

I have **compliments**.

Who has the missing word in this sentence: It was so ____ of him to share his grapes with his friends.

Vocabulary in Context 1

I have **generous**.

Who has the missing word in this sentence: Nadia had to ____ that she broke the glass.

I have **glance**.

Who has the missing word in this sentence: Carmen's aunt did not ____ her with her new haircut.

I have **admit**.

Who has the missing word in this sentence: Whom should we ask for ____ if we get lost?

I have **recognize**.

Who has the missing word in this sentence: There was such an ____ smell of perfume that Hilary couldn't stop sneezing.

I have **directions**.

Who has the missing word in this sentence: I'd like to ____ you to our new student.

I have **intense**.

Who has the missing word in this sentence: Greg lives in a two-story ____.

I have **introduce**.

Who has the missing word in this sentence: Let's go for a ____ through the garden.

I have **condominium**.

Who has the missing word in this sentence: Will you please ____ of this stinky trash?

I have **stroll**.

Who has the missing word in this sentence: Diana took a quick ____ at the new car in the window then walked on.

I have **dispose**.

Who has the missing word in this sentence: During the sale, she got a 25% ____ off all purchases.

Vocabulary in Context 1

I have **discount**. Who has the missing word in this sentence: She was hoping the ugly bruise would ____ quickly.	I have **attend**. Who has the missing word in this sentence: The bike was ____, so she didn't have to worry about falling off.
I have **vanish**. Who has the missing word in this sentence: The commercial was ____ the new toothpaste.	I have **stationary**. Who has the missing word in this sentence: At the ____ of the concert, the curtain went down.
I have **advertising**. Who has the missing word in this sentence: He was so full of ____ that he cleaned his room.	I have **conclusion**. Who has the missing word in this sentence: The hotel visitors were in a ____ when the alarm went off during the night.
I have **boredom**. Who has the missing word in this sentence: He gave his ____ for the ear medicine to the pharmacist.	I have **panic**. Who has the missing word in this sentence: I need to ____ some more money into my savings account.
I have **prescription**. Who has the missing word in this sentence: Do you plan to ____ the fund-raiser next week?	I have **deposit**. Who has the missing word in this sentence: We need to ____ for an earthquake by making an emergency kit.

Vocabulary in Context 1

I have **prepare**.

Who has the missing word in this sentence: Did you remember to make our ____ at the restaurant for 8:00?

I have **brave**.

Who has the missing word in this sentence: Did you have ____ to sleep over my house this weekend?

I have **reservation**.

Who has the missing word in this sentence: No student can beat her, so she is the chess ____ in her class.

I have **permission**.

Who has the missing word in this sentence: She was so honest that she couldn't ____ the fact that she forgot to set her alarm clock.

I have **champion**.

Who has the missing word in this sentence: I am ____ to begin my vacation.

I have **deny**.

Who has the missing word in this sentence: He entered the contest although he was ____ that he would win.

I have **eager**.

Who has the missing word in this sentence: There was a ____ against the player for starting an argument.

I have **doubtful**.

Who has the missing word in this sentence: Now it's time to ____ the eggs with the flour and mix it all together.

I have **penalty**.

Who has the missing word in this sentence: She tried to be ____ when she got the fifteen stitches.

I have **combine**.

Who has the first card?

Vocabulary in Context 1

Follow the path by highlighting the answers as your classmates identify them.

START *	MEADOW	PASSAGE	FURIOUS	DELICATE
INTRODUCE	DIRECTIONS	ADMIT	CALCULATE	DISAPPOINTED
STROLL	GLANCE	GENEROUS	UNFAIR	PROUD
ARTIFICIAL	RECOGNIZE	COMPLIMENTS	GREEDY	IDENTICAL
IMMENSE	INTENSE	CONDOMINIUM	DISPOSE	DISCOUNT
DEPOSIT	PANIC	CONCLUSION	STATIONARY	VANISH
PREPARE	NAUGHTY	OBSTACLE	ATTEND	ADVERTISING
RESERVATION	PERMISSION	DENY	PRESCRIPTION	BOREDOM
CHAMPION	BRAVE	DOUBTFUL	REGISTRATION	EVIDENCE
EAGER	PENALTY	**FINISH** * COMBINE	DEFEND	COOPERATE

Look at the words you did **not** highlight. Use each vocabulary word in a complete sentence. Use a dictionary, if needed.

1. ______________________________

2. ______________________________

3. ______________________________

4. ______________________________

5. ______________________________

6. ______________________________

7. ______________________________

8. ______________________________

9. ______________________________

10. ______________________________

Vocabulary in Context 2

I have the **first card**.

Who has the missing word in this sentence: It's a ____ restroom, so anyone can use it.

I have **estimate**.

Who has the missing word in this sentence: A rare species is not your ____ bird.

I have **public**.

Who has the missing word in this sentence: Did you hear about the $200 ____ for the missing cat?

I have **typical**.

Who has the missing word in this sentence: The trophies were on ____ in his bedroom.

I have **reward**.

Who has the missing word in this sentence: You spun a three so you can ____ three spaces on the gameboard.

I have **display**.

Who has the missing word in this sentence: What do you think lies ahead in your ____?

I have **advance**.

Who has the missing word in this sentence: I just learned the ____ of this new tool.

I have **future**.

Who has the missing word in this sentence: Now let's ____ to the next room on the tour.

I have **purpose**.

Who has the missing word in this sentence: I would ____ the total to be around ten dollars.

I have **proceed**.

Who has the missing word in this sentence: She was exaggerating her part in the play so she seemed so ____.

Vocabulary in Context 2

I have **dramatic**.

Who has the missing word in this sentence: His throat was so sore that he could ____ talk.

I have **concentrate**.

Who has the missing word in this sentence: She and her ____ enjoyed the trip.

I have **barely**.

Who has the missing word in this sentence: Do you think raising your hand is good classroom ____?

I have **companion**.

Who has the missing word in this sentence: I knew I could count on you to help. You are so ____.

I have **behavior**.

Who has the missing word in this sentence: You need to ____ me with your address and phone number.

I have **dependable**.

Who has the missing word in this sentence: Do I need to ____ you to study for your test?

I have **provide**.

Who has the missing word in this sentence: It's a unique ____ to train as an astronaut.

I have **remind**.

Who has the missing word in this sentence: Keisha keeps studying so she can ____ her good grades.

I have **opportunity**.

Who has the missing word in this sentence: He was trying to ____ on his studies, but the music was too loud.

I have **maintain**.

Who has the missing word in this sentence: The garden was colorful because of the ____ of flowers.

Vocabulary in Context 2

I have **variety**.

Who has the missing word in this sentence: Since we don't agree, I think we should ____ on which movie to watch.

I have **defective**.

Who has the missing word in this sentence: In which subject do you think you ____ the most?

I have **compromise**.

Who has the missing word in this sentence: You are under no ____ to help, but I would appreciate it if you did.

I have **excel**.

Who has the missing word in this sentence: The driver tried to ____ the items that fell out of the truck in front of him.

I have **obligation**.

Who has the missing word in this sentence: Without furniture, the room looked so ____.

I have **dodge**.

Who has the missing word in this sentence: She ____ tossed the laundry into the hamper, so it ended up on the floor instead.

I have **spacious**.

Who has the missing word in this sentence: Mark likes to ____ about the size of the fish he caught.

I have **carelessly**.

Who has the missing word in this sentence: We have one seat available since someone ____ their reservation.

I have **exaggerate**.

Who has the missing word in this sentence: If the radio is not working, it may have a ____ battery.

I have **cancelled**.

Who has the missing word in this sentence: Gina's ____ description of the car helped the police locate the stolen car.

Vocabulary in Context 2

I have **accurate**.

Who has the missing word in this sentence: I cannot ____ enough how important it is to eat breakfast.

I have **demonstrate**.

Who has the missing word in this sentence: You must ____ your dog's behavior when taking it for a walk.

I have **emphasize**.

Who has the missing word in this sentence: Were you able to ____ your parents to let you go with me to the zoo?

I have **monitor**.

Who has the missing word in this sentence: Hailey ____ visits her grandma and often sees her at least twice a week.

I have **persuade**.

Who has the missing word in this sentence: She had so much ____ that she was asked to be on a television show.

I have **frequently**.

Who has the missing word in this sentence: The ____ cooked a delicious pasta dish.

I have **talent**.

Who has the missing word in this sentence: It's rude to ____ people when they talk to you.

I have **chef**.

Who has the missing word in this sentence: Did you pay for your ____ with cash or a credit card?

I have **ignore**.

Who has the missing word in this sentence: The scientist dropped a ball to ____ how gravity works.

I have **merchandise**.

Who has the first card?

Vocabulary in Context 2

Follow the path by highlighting the vocabulary words as your classmates identify them.

LIMITED	SUCCESSFUL	**FINISH** * MERCHANDISE	CHEF
PERSIST	DEMONSTRATE	MONITOR	FREQUENTLY
TALENT	IGNORE	DODGE	EXCEL
PERSUADE	CANCELLED	CARELESSLY	DEFECTIVE
EMPHASIZE	ACCURATE	SPACIOUS	EXAGGERATE
VARIETY	COMPROMISE	OBLIGATION	ENCOURAGE
MAINTAIN	TYPICAL	ESTIMATE	PURPOSE
REMIND	DISPLAY	FUTURE	ADVANCE
DEPENDABLE	COMPANION	PROCEED	REWARD
OPPORTUNITY	CONCENTRATE	DRAMATIC	PUBLIC
PROVIDE	BEHAVIOR	BARELY	**START** *

Look at the boxes you did **not** highlight. Use each vocabulary word in a complete sentence. Use a dictionary, if needed.

1. ______________________________

2. ______________________________

3. ______________________________

4. ______________________________

Choose five words that describe you. Use each word in a sentence that explains why you think that word describes you.

5. ______________________________

6. ______________________________

7. ______________________________

8. ______________________________

9. ______________________________

Answer Key

Synonyms 1 (Page 10)

START *	COMPANION	PRESENT	FINISH * RECALL	DIFFICULT
CONCLUDE	FEARSOME	CONSIDERATE	GIGANTIC	ACCOMPLISH
OPINION	RELAXED	DANGEROUS	CLOSE	EDUCATE
ACCURATE	IDEAS	BRAVE	ENORMOUS	RICH
REQUEST	ANNOY	PITY	PRETTY	QUICK
PERSUADE	AID	CLEAN	WISH	SLOW
DEMAND	START	SIMPLE	LEAVE	HUMOROUS
ANSWER	PAUSE	RUSH	ARRIVE	PURCHASE
ALTER	COLLECT	SHORT	ARTIFICIAL	SICK
PLEDGE	RESULT	TENSION	DESTROYED	GLAD

Answers will vary. Possible answers include:

1. companion—friend
2. difficult—hard
3. brave—courageous
4. enormous—huge
5. pity—shame
6. aid—help
7. slow—sluggish
8. rush—hurry
9. arrive—appear
10. collect—gather

Synonyms 2 (Page 15)

→CAUTION	WICKED	ACCURATE	GREEDY
INEXPENSIVE	ENTERTAIN	SINCERITY	LEAVE
RARE	JUDGMENT	GONE	BEGIN
ARTIFICIAL	ORGANIZED	DOUBT	CLEAN
GIVING	TEAR	AWARD	UNJUST
TOXIC	CONSTRUCT	TARDY	SPEAK
TREMBLE	COLLECT	ASSIST	MATERIALS
FORETELL	PETITE	SECTION	INTELLIGENT
CRUSH	TENANT	TOUGH	VOW
FAMILIAR	PERSON	NOTICE	SMART
A	B	C	D

Answers will vary. Possible answers include:

1. accurate—right
2. sincerity—truthfulness
3. gone—left
4. doubt—suspect
5. award—reward
6. tardy—delayed
7. assist—aid
8. section—part
9. tough—challenging
10. notice—view

Synonyms 3 (Page 20)

BECAUSE	TRAIL	RESPECT	BASHFUL	OPTIMISTIC
CUTE	HARMED	CURRENT	ASTONISHED	CRUEL
ATTRACTIVE	REVISE	IT	CONQUER	GENUINE
FALSE	POSSESS	SEAT	EXPENSIVE	PREDICT
DEFINITELY	DESIRE	UPSET	HAPPY	EMPTY
STRONG	DESCRIBE	TOW	IMITATE	QUIET
HAD	HELPFUL	CREATE	LEAVE	PAIL
LARGE	RUIN	SNOOZE	A	APPLAUD
ANSWER	RIDICULOUS	CONCEAL	CLEAN	FINISH * STOP
START *	STARE	THROW	VIRUS	SMART

Riddle: Because it had a virus!

Answers will vary. Possible answers include:

1. cute—attractive
2. happy—glad
3. helpful—useful
4. clean—sanitary
5. smart—intelligent

Synonyms 4 (Page 25)

A	E	E	M	P	L	O	Y	F	I	N	I	S	H	I	N	D	O	O	R	S
G	R	I	M	Y	C	L	O	S	E	D	S	P	R	I	M	U	U	W	E	C
L	E	T	H	A	L	A	E	I	O	I	I	E	U	I	L	N	O	O	X	A
E	O	O	B	S	E	R	V	E	A	S	M	T	O	N	A	O	I	R	P	S
T	H	A	W	M	E	S	S	Y	I	C	P	T	I	S	T	R	E	T	E	H
P	O	O	I	N	S	P	E	C	T	O	L	Y	P	I	E	G	A	H	N	N
O	S	A	V	E	O	D	A	U	I	V	E	E	E	S	G	A	E	W	S	U
S	T	H	A	S	I	I	I	S	E	E	A	P	R	T	R	N	X	H	E	M
I	A	E	I	E	O	F	L	E	A	R	C	U	M	O	A	I	H	I	E	E
T	R	L	I	L	E	F	L	F	F	A	C	R	I	O	T	Z	A	L	A	R
I	D	P	O	E	O	E	I	U	R	E	U	S	T	A	E	E	U	E	S	O
V	Y	E	A	C	O	R	R	L	A	I	S	U	E	E	F	D	S	U	A	U
E	U	R	A	T	A	E	E	U	I	O	E	E	E	I	U	O	T	O	M	S
S	P	L	I	T	I	N	P	A	D	R	A	P	I	D	L	A	E	I	P	S
M	O	N	E	Y	E	T	A	E	A	E	I	O	Y	E	L	L	D	E	L	T
D	I	S	T	A	N	T	I	S	M	A	R	T	S	I	L	L	Y	A	E	A
C	L	E	V	E	R	U	R	O	S	A	C	K	A	D	I	N	N	E	R	Y
U	O	A	I	P	O	L	I	S	H	A	A	A	F	O	E	S	I	C	K	A

1. c
2. e
3. f
4. a
5. b
6. d

Antonyms 1 (Page 30)

BORING	DISTANT	FICTION	FINISH * IMMATURE	COMICAL
REPAIR	DEADLY	LEAVE	DIVIDE	GLOSSY
REWARD	NOVICE	SEPARATE	REVEAL	PRIVATE
INITIAL	PEACEFUL	SAFE	CURVED	AHEAD
START *	NOISY	ASHAMED	FAILURE	EFFECT
LOCATE	MEAN	SAVE	BORROW	HEALTHY
LOSE	SIMPLE	OMIT	END	ORGANIZED
EXIT	SUCCEED	OPINION	ANSWER	DRY
SELL	AGREE	DENY	TRAP	DECREASE
ROUGH	ARRIVE	LOWER	FORTUNATE	CLUMSY

Answers will vary. Possible answers include:

1. comical—tragic
2. deadly—harmless
3. leave—arrive
4. divide—combine
5. glossy—dull
6. initial—final
7. peaceful—violent
8. simple—difficult
9. succeed—fail
10. rough—smooth

Antonyms 2 (Page 35)

→	NOW	FUTURE	SHOUT
ENDANGER	INSIDE	STUDENT	DISLOYAL
RECEIVE	UNKNOWN	MISPLACE	LEAD
SWEET	EXTERIOR	NOBODY	COMPREHEND
ANCIENT	FORGET	PROMPT	POVERTY
UNIQUE	THICK	EVENING	UNCERTAIN
ABNORMAL	IGNORE	PRESENT	REVEALED
CEASE	GUILTY	FEEBLE	TAINTED
HARSH	DISTANT	CLARIFY	EXPERT
REJECT	WHOLE	COMPLIMENT	HUMBLE
A	B	C	D

Answers will vary. Possible answers include:

1. now—formerly
2. inside—outdoor
3. unknown—known
4. exterior—internal
5. forget—memorize
6. thick—slender
7. ignore—notice
8. guilty—blameless
9. distant—close
10. whole—section

Antonyms 3 (Page 40)

START *	INCOMPLETE	HELPFUL	HURT	FILL
PERSEVERE	BELOW	REVEAL	MOUNTAIN	FINISH * NORMAL
VERTICAL	POLLUTE	DAMAGE	MAJOR	POLITE
CATCH	COWARDLY	THEY	TIGHT	KEEP
APPROXIMATE	SILLY	INCLUDE	MAXIMUM	IT
REPEL	COUNTERFEIT	CONTRACT	IN	SNOW
SOOTHE	BANKS	UGLY	STALE	TARDY
SADNESS	DEADLY	SUBTRACTION	SMOOTH	COUNTERCLOCKWISE
BLEND	EASY	INACTIVE	AVOID	DAWN
SHRINK	USEFUL	AGED	FREED	ORGANIZED

Riddle: They keep it in snow banks!

Answers will vary. Possible answers include:

1. helpful—unhelpful
2. polite—rude
3. tardy—early
4. organized—messy

Antonyms 4 (Page 45)

D	A	D	E	I	P	D	E	F	E	C	T	I	V	E	H	U	N	G	R	Y	O
I	F	I	X	D	U	G	O	S	O	F	T	P	E	A	C	E	F	U	L	F	I
F	U	S	H	E	L	U	L	O	O	B	U	S	Y	A	R	I	V	A	L	A	T
F	L	C	A	C	L	E	E	R	E	L	E	A	S	E	W	O	R	S	T	L	E
I	L	O	U	A	R	S	A	L	A	I	L	L	E	G	A	L	C	I	A	L	N
C	A	U	S	Y	E	S	D	A	E	R	O	T	T	E	N	A	O	M	J	I	S
U	F	R	T	R	J	E	A	N	E	S	E	R	I	O	U	S	M	P	O	N	E
L	U	A	E	E	E	E	O	D	S	T	I	N	K	Y	A	C	B	R	L	G	E
T	N	G	D	M	C	O	I	S	I	M	P	L	E	A	U	A	I	O	L	I	E
O	N	E	S	E	T	D	E	C	E	A	S	E	D	U	I	N	N	V	Y	I	A
R	Y	S	H	M	F	I	E	A	I	A	E	L	E	S	S	C	E	E	O	D	D
E	I	E	A	B	R	O	A	O	A	U	A	L	O	A	N	E	D	Q	O	A	R
M	F	L	L	E	E	A	W	I	N	F	E	R	I	O	R	L	U	U	I	F	O
O	A	L	L	R	S	U	I	I	O	A	E	I	O	U	A	E	L	I	U	L	U
V	C	O	O	A	H	O	L	E	A	U	N	E	V	E	N	E	L	T	O	A	G
E	E	I	W	E	A	I	D	A	I	M	P	R	O	B	A	B	L	E	I	T	H
S	H	A	R	E	F	O	O	L	I	S	H	N	E	S	S	I	I	D	L	E	O

1. d
2. f
3. a
4. b
5. c
6. e

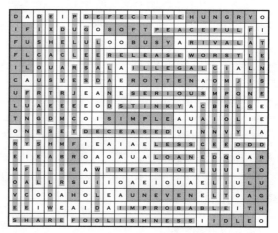

Homophone Riddles (Page 50)

LONE LOAN	CREWS' CRUISE	CEILING SEALING	I HEARD A HERD	CREEK CREAK	FINISH * MALE MAIL
DEAR DEER	ROSE ROWS	BARE BEAR	FLOWER FLOUR	KNIGHT NIGHT	COARSE COURSE
BLUE BLEW	KNEW NEW	TAIL TALE	EYE I	SEE SEA	WEIGHT WAIT
AUNT ANT	HOARSE HORSE	MISSED MIST	STEAL STEEL	HIGH HI	HARE HAIR
START *	POLL POLE	CHEAP CHEEP	MEAT MEET	OUR HOUR	WHOLE HOLE
SWEET SUITE	BEAT BEET	REAL REEL	BEACH BEECH	TACKS TAX	CENT SCENT
FOUL FOWL	FLEE FLEA	WAIST WASTE	MAID MADE	PALE PAIL	BYE BUY
DOE WITH DOUGH	BORED BOARD	WRITE RIGHT	RODE ROAD	MEET MEAT	PAWS PAUSE
FAIR FARE	I ATE EIGHT	WEAK WEEK	TOWED TOAD	PLAIN PLANE	SCENE SEEN

blue	blew	maid	made
eye	I	write	right
weight	wait	scene	seen
meat	meet		

Homophone Spelling (Page 55)

START →	BEAR	STEAL	TO
RAINS	WASTE	HAIR	MALE
TEA	THERE	MEAT	WRITE
WEAK	KNOT	MAID	PAIL
HOLE	KNEW	HEAR	PIECE
TWO	HERE	MAIL	MEET
THEIR	REINS	RIGHT	MADE
WHOLE	TOO	HARE	WAIST
STEEL	BARE	WEEK	NOT
PALE	NEW	TEE	CENT
A	B	C	D

1. to	two or too
2. male	mail
3. write	right
4. pail	pale
5. piece	peace
6. meet	meat
7. made	maid
8. waist	waste
9. not	knot
10. cent	scent

Compound Words (Page 60)

START →	ROAD	SPREAD	SHAKE
MATE	LACE	SHIP	CASE
KNOB	PAPER	QUAKE	CORN
CRACKER	GOWN	BOX	MEAL
DAY	WISE	SIDE	BOARD
BOOK	CAKE	POT	TOP
PIECE	SAND	BOAT	BACK
MOWER	ACHE	STORM	PASTE
STOOL	BUG	DOWN	BASKET
COLOR	CROW	COAT	SCRAPER
A	B	C	D

1. milk + shake = milkshake
2. suit + case = suitcase
3. pop + corn = popcorn
4. oat + meal = oatmeal
5. cup + board = cupboard
6. black + top = blacktop
7. horse + back = horseback
8. tooth + paste = toothpaste
9. waste + basket = wastebasket
10. sky + scraper = skyscraper

Compound Word Jokes (Page 65)

START *	THE MOCKINGBIRD IS ALWAYS MOCKING HIM	THE CARPOOL	CATFISH
A WATCHDOG	HE WANTED TO PUT OUT HIS HEARTBURN	BECAUSE HIS SNOWSHOES MELTED	HE WANTED TO SEE THE FISHBOWL
THEY WANTED TO HAVE A GRASSHOPPER	HE WANTED TO PLAY HIS EARDRUMS	SHE WANTED TO HAVE A COPYCAT	SHE WANTED TO CATCH STARFISH
SHE WANTED TO SEE A GUMDROP	FINGERNAILS	HORSESHOE	RAILROAD
THE BOOKKEEPER	SEAHORSES	AN EGGROLL	FINISH * AN ANTEATER
IT WAS A BLUEBERRY	POPCORN	A BULLDOZER	ROADMAP
APPLESAUCE	SHOELACE	THE FOXTROT	REDBIRD
THE CROW THOUGHT IT WAS IN A BIRDHOUSE	CARHOP	A GROUNDHOG	BACKYARD
SHE WANTED TO HEAR HER EARRING	BLACKBERRY	A BULLFROG	SPACESHIP
HE DIDN'T WANT TO GET CARSICK	HOUSEFLY	BECAUSE THEY WEAR SNOWCAPS	WHEN YOU EAT A WATERMELON
HE WANTED TO GET EGGSHELLS	HE WANTED A PLAYSTATION	TEACUP	JELLYFISH
IN SNOWBANKS	FROSTBITE	HEADLIGHT	A BELLYBUTTON
A WEBSITE	MILKSHAKES	MICROWAVES	LAWSUITS
A RAINBOW	SPRINGTIME	SUNLIGHT	COUNTRYSIDE

Sentences will vary.

Making Compound Words (Page 70)

START →	SUN	AIR	SOME
EYE	BLUE	HOME	HEAD
HOUSE	SEA	SAND	HONEY
TOOTH	RAIN	SUPER	SOME
ANY	BACK	UNDER	BOOK
LIFE	FORE	THUMB	BLACK
DAY	CAR	GRAND	SIDE
NEWS	SNOW	TIME	TABLE
SHORT	PIG	FIRE	FLOWER
OUT	PINE	RACE	TEA
A	B	C	D

Answers will vary.

Nouns (Page 75)

C	A	M	P	G	R	O	U	N	D	H	N	O	U	S	I	G	N
T	N	T	C	L	O	W	N	S	P	O	M	O	T	O	R	C	M
R	O	R	N	B	N	C	O	C	O	U	S	T	O	V	E	A	O
E	V	U	U	O	N	A	F	A	O	S	D	R	E	A	M	R	U
E	E	C	N	O	O	R	A	R	L	E	C	E	R	E	A	L	S
H	L	K	U	K	N	R	B	P	R	A	D	I	O	D	N	T	E
O	T	O	W	E	R	O	R	E	O	U	N	N	O	U	U	O	N
U	N	O	U	C	N	T	I	T	P	U	P	P	Y	C	S	W	J
S	N	T	O	A	U	S	C	F	A	R	M	E	R	K	C	E	A
E	R	E	N	V	M	O	N	E	Y	N	O	U	S	S	H	R	C
W	E	L	N	E	P	A	I	N	T	I	N	G	H	N	O	B	K
A	P	E	T	O	C	A	L	E	N	D	A	R	O	U	O	E	E
T	O	V	R	B	O	O	K	N	N	O	U	N	E	N	L	E	T
C	R	I	A	O	M	S	T	R	A	W	B	E	R	R	I	E	S
H	T	S	S	G	O	C	A	R	P	E	N	T	E	R	W	P	T
B	U	I	H	L	V	N	H	N	O	P	L	A	N	E	A	A	R
A	U	O	N	O	I	N	A	B	A	L	L	O	O	N	T	P	E
N	O	N	U	V	E	N	N	A	N	I	M	A	L	N	E	E	E
D	O	U	N	E	N	O	D	R	A	B	B	I	T	U	R	R	N
N	O	U	C	O	O	K	I	E	N	B	A	S	E	B	A	L	L

Sentences will vary.

Adjectives (Page 80)

→	TINY	CURLY	NARROW
SILENT	BROKEN	LITTLE	CUDDLY
SLOW	NOISY	FEW	MANY
DAMAGED	DRY	PETITE	FLUFFY
JUICY	NERVOUS	STICKY	MYSTERIOUS
FUNNY	STALE	WICKED	MASSIVE
EMPTY	SCREECHING	FOOLISH	COURAGEOUS
TASTY	MELTED	ANGRY	CROOKED
CREEPY	LATE	SPICY	LOOSE
STRONG	HUNGRY	CONFUSED	GREASY
A	B	C	D

Sentences will vary.

Verbs (Page 85)

CLIMB	START *	ATE	DRINK	WATCH	CLIMB
BUY	READ	DEBATED	OWNS	EMPLOYS	FINISH * ESTIMATED
DRIVES	BREAK	BUILT	DESCRIBE	INTERVIEWED	DESERVE
DESIGNED	LANDED	LISTED	ADOPTED	COMPUTE	CAN TRACE
FREEZES	COOK	WRITE	RETELL	WILL DISCUSS	DRAW
ESCAPED	EXPIRES	SAY	EXAMINED	COMPARE	INVENTED
EXPLAIN	RECOVER	PLANTING	CHOOSE	TRANSLATE	WILL RETIRE
RAISE	WADDLED	ASSISTED	DROVE	HELPING	ARE CREEPING
WANDERED	PASSED	RODE	COME	HUNG	PURCHASED

Sentences will vary.

Adverbs (Page 90)

→	KINDLY	QUIETLY	TRUTHFULLY
FOOLISHLY	NEATLY	SUDDENLY	LAZILY
ACCIDENTALLY	DAILY	SELFISHLY	WARMLY
SAFELY	REALLY	NERVOUSLY	FAR
RARELY	LOUDLY	CAUTIOUSLY	CORRECTLY
CALMLY	ELEGANTLY	CHEERFULLY	THOUGHTFULLY
LESS	OFTEN	POLITELY	GENTLY
SELDOM	SUCCESSFULLY	CAREFULLY	BRIEFLY
PROMPTLY	OBEDIENTLY	RUDELY	VIOLENTLY
ALMOST	FAIRLY	GRACEFULLY	SADLY
A	B	C	D

Sentences will vary.

Collective Nouns (Page 95)

TEAM	BED	CLUSTER	RANGE	PRIDE	POD
HORDE	CAST	BELT	FLEET	STREAK	PLATOON
GAGGLE	SCHOOL	STRING	TROUPE	CHAIN	STAFF
BUNCH	PACK	BROOD	ATLAS	CLASS	TEAM
HERD	LITTER	BOUQUET	CREW	BAND	CROWD
FLOCK	SWARM	QUIVER	CACHE	CARAVAN	FLIGHT
ARMY	COLONY	RING	PANEL	BATCH	LIBRARY
START *	TRIBE	ROOKERY	LIST FINISH*	DECK	NETWORK

1. cluster—grasshoppers, spiders
2. streak—tigers
3. string—pearls, beads
4. troupe—performers
5. bunch—flowers
6. brood—chickens
7. atlas—maps
8. band—gorillas, men

Tenses—Past, Present, or Future? (Page 100)

We have seven pet rabbits.	He broke his arm when he fell off the mountain.	The cookies will be ready in five minutes.
The apples were picked last week.	She went shopping last night.	We took so many pictures of our vacation.
Will your baby be a boy or a girl?	This is the best vacation I have ever had!	The new socks will be ordered from the Internet company.
The turtle won the race.	You will break your arm if you climb that mountain!	They left early this morning to go camping.
Why are there so many ants here?	They will be coming home from the camping trip.	The table will be used for the family dinner.
The waves on the lake are so smooth.	It all started three months ago with two rabbits.	Look! Is that really a turtle trying to cross the road?
The oranges will be ripe in two weeks.	The leg of the table broke during dinner.	We found the lake last year while on vacation.
Start *	Are the cookies burning?	We will play your soccer team next week.
The baby cried.	I lost my socks last week at camp.	The doctor is placing the boy's broken arm in a cast.
They are playing soccer at the park.	I will be leaving for my vacation next week.	Will our next door neighbors go on the picnic too?
Where will your cruise ship go?	This hamburger is delicious.	Are you enjoying your first camping trip?
The ants were all over the picnic table!	The baby rabbits should be born in the next few days.	Please pass the apples.
My baby is a girl.	She accidentally burned the cookies.	I am working on my project.
She ate all of her vegetables.	The lake will be closed for the winter.	We will go to the zoo tomorrow.
Both of my socks have holes in them!	The table looks so lovely tonight.	They donated cans to the food bank.
The turtle should cross the road by noon.	Finish * My team won the soccer game.	They will be eating at the restaurant around the corner.

1. past
2. future
3. present
4. present
5. past
6. future
7. past
8. future

Prefixes and Suffixes (Page 105)

A	B	C	D
START →	AUTO-	INTER-	DE-
EX-	POST-	BI-	SYM-
DIS-	BIO-	UN-	IR-
POLY-	MONO-	MICRO-	SUB-
CONTRA-	MAL-	TELE-	RE-
TRANS-	PRE-	PHOTO-	IN-
OB-	MIS-	IM-	TRI-
CO-	SUPER-	CENTI-	-ABLE
-OR	-OLOGY	-LESS	-IST
-PHOBIA	-EST	-IFY	-ER

1. de-; from
2. sym-; together
3. ir-; not
4. sub-; under
5. re-; again
6. in-; not
7. tri-; three
8. -able; capable, able to be
9. -ist; one who does something
10. -er; one who does something

Greek and Latin Roots (Page 110)

A	B	C	D
START →	SPECT	SOL	DICT
GRESS	JECT	PEL	PORT
SCRIBE	TRACT	VERT	PEND
CHROME	DEM	PHON	CHRON
PHIL	PATH	AUDI	MIT
FRACT	MEM	PED	LIBER
CREAT	CENT	VIS	THERM
ASTRO	GRAPH	JUNC	DERM
AMBI	ARCH	JUR	PAR
VIT	TELE	VAC	VOL

1. spect; to see
2. ject; to throw
3. tract; to pull
4. dem; people
5. path; feeling or suffering
6. mem; keep in mind
7. cent; one hundred
8. graph; writing
9. arch; rule
10. tele; far away

Base Words (Page 115)

M	T	P	A	J	U	D	G	E	M	I	G	R	A	T	E	D	O	W
O	O	L	D	I	R	E	C	T	S	C	A	E	I	B	A	K	E	I
B	X	E	L	D	A	T	E	A	M	R	R	E	F	U	S	E	M	S
I	I	A	I	A	G	R	E	E	A	A	U	P	O	W	E	R	A	E
L	N	S	G	A	E	I	A	U	R	C	S	T	R	O	N	G	R	D
E	F	E	H	H	A	P	P	Y	T	K	A	R	R	I	V	E	I	E
A	R	A	T	U	N	D	E	R	S	T	A	N	D	A	E	D	N	P
P	O	A	E	O	P	E	N	W	A	T	E	S	T	A	E	R	E	E
P	S	C	H	A	N	G	E	E	O	P	E	R	A	T	E	I	F	N
E	T	A	C	T	I	I	O	E	E	N	O	R	M	A	L	V	R	D
A	T	H	R	O	N	E	A	K	E	P	C	Y	C	L	E	E	E	W
R	A	B	E	L	I	E	V	E	A	A	A	B	R	A	V	E	S	O
A	N	G	L	E	H	A	P	P	Y	I	S	P	E	L	L	A	H	R
O	U	C	O	M	F	O	R	T	U	D	P	E	R	F	E	C	T	K

Answers will vary.

Alphabetical Order (Page 120)

LACK	FALSE	MORE	SHELL	DARK	DRIP	LODGE	CHEW
SHELF	MEND	DOG	CODE	COVER	SMILE	HAPPY	TOE
BARLEY	RANGE	DARE	LAW	PART	FIGHT	WASTE	SCARE
START *	BACKBONE	BAG	STOVE	LOFT	DENT	LIFT	GARDEN
HEAD	MUTTER	RAPID	FEED	MILL	CLEAN	WATER	TRAY
JOKE	CHOOSE	WHEAT	CHEF	HIP	GLUE	PLANE	LONG
FINISH *	GIRL	CASE	CHASE	JAR	ORANGE	TREAT	CLAP

barley
case
chef
clean
dark
girl
head
mutter
orange
part
plane
range
rapid
scare
smile

Rhyme Time 1 (Page 125)

START →	PLAYED	REPRESENT	BROOK
RESIDENTIAL	DIVIDED	GRIM	LENDING
EACH	PROMOTE	BEAUTY	SHEEP
CONCERN	PUFF	FULL	DEW
PRESSED	FORGOTTEN	SNEEZE	CONVERT
DISAGREE	ASTOUND	SCHOLAR	TURKEY
HURRY	DIZZY	DEFAULT	SOUVENIR
CHARTER	SQUIRT	DECEIVE	INHALE
SHAKE	MARSH	DISASTER	CABOOSE
EAGLE	ATTENTION	CREATURE	BABOON
A	B	C	D

Answers will vary.

Rhyme Time 2 (Page 130)

FUNNY MONEY	CLEAN QUEEN	HOT POT	JEWEL FUEL	MOWED ROAD
WEE BEE	SLIME CRIME	BRAVE SAVE	CRACKED FACT	FINISH* BLACK PLAQUE
HOLLOW SWALLOW	CRUEL DUEL	MOUSE HOUSE	ROSE NOSE	DAMP LAMP
BEAR STARE	GRAND BAND	SHOWER HOUR	DREAM SCREAM	BLACK SACK
START *	CITY PITY	FAT CAT	GLAD PAD	SWEET MEAT
SMART HEART	SQUID KID	GHOST TOAST	NOODLE POODLE	LATE BAIT
RARE PAIR	RIPPED SCRIPT	SWIFT GIFT	NEAT BEAT	SAD LAD
SLUMBER LUMBER	COLD GOLD	BLURRED WORD	WIZARD LIZARD	SORE DOOR
SAD DAD	BOOK COOK	OCEAN POTION	THROWN STONE	GAG RAG
CROSS SAUCE	LATE DEBATE	CREATURE TEACHER	BLESSED TEST	PLAIN TRAIN

Answers will vary.

Multiple-Meaning Words 1 (Page 135)

Start *	I need to pack my suitcase for the trip.	She will color her hair light pink.
We like to pet puppies.	He pounded the post deep into the ground.	It's time for a lunch break.
It's time to spring out of bed!	How does the pasta taste?	It's rude to point at people.
Where is his new place located?	It's time to go to the grocery store.	I'll help you crack the walnuts.
Are you ready for me to deal the cards?	I'll have your car repaired in a snap.	Who would like to raise the flag?
Did you dress the baby yet?	He put a dark finish on the wood cabinet.	I acted like such a fool.
They ran three laps around the track.	Cara tried to shape the clay into a vase.	I taught my ferret how to roll over.
Try not to bend the edges of the book.	Where is the wood for the fire?	It takes hard work to master a skill.
Her desk was in the corner of her room.	He had a cut on his toe.	You need to report your grades to your mother.
Would you like me to shine your shoes?	The boat was supposed to float.	It's smart to face your fears.
She needed to fast for two days.	Mr. Jones will post the grades.	The roses grew tall in the potting soil.
You should brush your teeth every day.	The water pumps are out of order.	Mia has to string the beads to make a necklace.
I placed a bowl of fruit on the table.	I need a tailor to patch these jeans.	Did you set the chickens free?
Is the car in gear?	Will you share those cookies with me?	Keep your eyes peeled for the sign.
I trust you to keep a secret.	There was a mouse in the garage.	She tried to reason with her father.
It's time to root for your favorite team.	The shirt was wrinkled, so she needed to press it.	Please play that note on your piano.
Look at how fast he can pitch!	A bat flew out of the cave.	FINISH * Try not to tip over the gameboard.

1. deal
2. dress
3. finish
4. face
5. fast
6. free
7. gear
8. peeled
9. reason
10. press
11. note

Multiple-Meaning Words 2 (Page 140)

What is the make of your new car?	Where did you park your car?	What does the price tag say?	Finish * They had to dig a well to get water for their country house.
What page are you on in your new book?	She tried to mold the dough into a loaf of bread.	First, he had to season the ribs with barbecue sauce.	We can watch television after dinner.
Remember to lock the door when you leave.	What's the matter with you today?	She put strawberry preserves on her toast.	How would you rate that book on a scale of 1 to 5?
She boiled the water on her cooktop range.	Mrs. Brown will stamp each student's paper.	The sound of the clock's ticks drove her crazy.	We need to wash the car.
I tend to spend too much money.	She wore a pink slip under her dress.	Did you wave goodbye to your friend?	Try not to stuff it all inside.
I put the new TV stand over there.	You can trace over each detail carefully.	The final pass led to a touchdown.	They saw many temples on their vacation.
The car had so much power!	Please draw a plane figure.	Did you squash that bug?	It was time to go to work.
That jacket is mine.	The litter was thrown away.	Grandma plays the organ on Sundays.	He had the lead in the school play.
Your bank account earns interest every month.	Will you please load the dryer for me?	I'll meet you at the theater at 8:00.	Where is the ground pepper?
She knocked on the door.	Are you a sports fan?	The baby has applesauce all over his face.	Which game would you like to play first?
He had a patch on the knee of his jeans.	You only need one application of shampoo to wash your hair.	Can you find the street on the map?	Did you flush the toilet?
Do you know how to pitch a tent?	You need to change your shoes.	The sign said, "Buy one, get one free."	You can form the line right here.
Start *	I like how you chose to accent the colors in your bedspread.	That's a sharp point on that pencil.	We need to pile into the van for the road trip.

1. make
2. preserves
3. rate
4. pass
5. power
6. plane
7. lead, play
8. ground
9. patch
10. pitch
11. point
12. pile

Analogies (Page 145)

D	E	S	K	P	O	O	D	L	E	N	T	A	K	E
A	H	A	N	G	A	R	S	O	L	I	D	N	A	L
F	O	O	T	O	E	P	A	I	N	T	G	Y	I	S
C	H	I	L	D	V	H	F	A	C	B	E	E	S	G
O	M	P	A	R	E	A	O	D	O	E	R	C	H	E
C	R	Y	N	O	N	M	O	I	S	O	N	O	E	N
O	F	L	O	U	I	S	T	S	K	I	N	F	X	E
M	W	O	U	N	N	T	B	M	O	Y	R	F	A	R
I	D	V	N	D	G	E	A	O	R	O	S	E	G	O
S	T	E	T	W	O	R	L	N	A	U	H	E	O	U
T	D	R	I	F	T	S	L	E	D	N	A	T	N	S
A	A	A	L	L	S	R	E	Y	I	G	H	E	A	D
K	W	A	L	L	T	R	B	E	O	S	L	E	E	P
E	S	L	H	A	R	T	A	V	A	C	U	U	M	S
T	H	M	O	E	I	W	K	R	O	A	R	D	I	N
R	E	O	L	N	N	E	E	S	E	C	O	N	D	O
E	E	O	E	S	G	T	S	C	H	O	O	L	O	W
E	P	N	W	O	R	D	M	E	W	A	Y	T	R	Y

1. take
2. try
3. moon
4. young
5. foot
6. hole

An analogy is a comparison of words that are related in some way.

Sentences—Declarative, Imperative, Interrogative, and Exclamatory (Page 150)

My favorite video game is broken!	I turned in my homework on time.	Finish * Ouch! His pencil poked me!	Where is the return bin for library books?
What kind of flowers did you plant in your garden?	Can we go to the carnival tomorrow?	Write your name on your homework.	There's a fly on my birthday cake!
Throw that soda can in the recycle bin.	The video game is on that table.	Is that your golden retriever?	The bubbles in the soda upset my stomach.
Will this rain ever stop?	What kind of frosting would you like on the cake?	What an exciting carnival ride!	Return that library book today.
The library is closed.	Oh no! The rain caused a mudslide!	I have roses in my garden.	She went to the park to enjoy a picnic.
My garden is so beautiful!	Sharpen your pencil before class.	Where is your homework?	Put the picnic basket over there.
Buy the tickets for the carnival.	That dog just bit me!	I'll use my new pencil.	Put that video game away right now.
When will we leave for the picnic?	Pick the tomatoes in the garden first.	My soda just spilled all over me!	Put the leash on your dog.
The ants are all over the picnic basket!	It's time to take my dog for a walk.	Don't lick the frosting before we cut the cake.	It's raining hard today.
My favorite dessert is chocolate cake.	Are you ready to play my new video game with me?	May I borrow a pencil?	This carnival is fun.
My library books are five days overdue!	Put on your raincoat.	Oh no! I lost my homework!	Start *

1. declarative—She went to the park to enjoy a picnic.
2. imperative—Put the picnic basket over there.
3. interrogative—When will we leave for the picnic?
4. exclamatory—The ants are all over the picnic basket!

Context Clues (Page 155)

FERTILE	ARGUMENT OR DISAGREEMENT	WORRY	SHY	PERSUADE
FINISH * JOURNEY	POISONOUS	MONEY EARNED	FALL DOWN DUE TO A LOSS OF STRENGTH	PUBLICATIONS
DISQUALIFIED	CONCEAL	SPEED UP	GUILTY PERSON	TELL OR REVEAL
FROM OTHER PLACES	PUT OUT	GREATLY DISLIKES	USELESS	GET
START *	GOOD FOR GROWING	SUPPORT	OUT OF USE OR OUT OF FASHION	SPEAK
HOAX	SERIOUS	TAKE APART	TRICK	FLEXIBLE
LOOKING AT	CONVINCE	HIDE	CAUTIOUS OR WATCHFUL	HOLD BACK
PUBLISHED WORKS	OBTAIN	FAKE NAME	NEXT TO OR NEAR	ENTHUSIASM
NEW AND UNUSUAL	GAME	EXCITED	STARED IN AMAZEMENT	WIN OR BE VICTORIOUS
CULPRIT	REMOVED OR KICKED OUT	MEDICINE	INCOME	TOXIC

Sentences will vary.

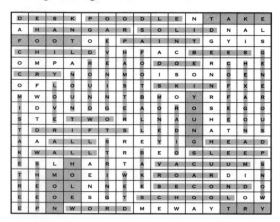

Main Idea and Details 1 (Page 160)

START*	MUSICAL INSTRUMENTS	THINGS THAT ARE BLUE	COLORS
REPTILES	FISH	FRUITS	SNAKES
BOARD GAMES	COMPUTERS	MAMMALS	SHAPES
COINS	THINGS YOU WEAR ON YOUR HEAD	AMPHIBIANS	FLOWERS
THINGS YOU DRINK	EXERCISE EQUIPMENT	TREES	BIRDS
ORGANS	FOREST ANIMALS	THINGS WE GET FROM ANIMALS	FARM ANIMALS
INSECTS	ANIMAL HOMES	AUTOMOBILES	VEGETABLES
EMOTIONS	THINGS YOU USE TO COOK	THINGS YOU READ	THINGS IN THE SKY
THINGS YOU WEAR ON YOUR FEET	BODIES OF WATER	SCHOOL SUBJECTS	WATER TRANSPORTATION VEHICLES
SNACKS	FLAVORS	WAYS TO MOVE	CAMPING GEAR
THINGS FOR A BABY FINISH *	THINGS AT A BIRTHDAY PARTY	THINGS THAT HOLD ITEMS TOGETHER	PARTS OF A BOOK

1. breeds of dogs
2. beverages
3. parts of a car
4. cheeses
5. breads
6. butterfly

Main Idea and Details 2 (Page 165)

A	B	C	D
START →	YELLOW	NIGHTLIGHT	REALISTIC FICTION
LIONS	SANDCASTLES	BUILDING MODEL CARS	FOCUS
CHICKEN POX	BANANAS	TERRIERS	TRIANGLE
DEVICE	MONTHS	EARRINGS	LINES
DISHWASHER	ROAST BEEF	MARSHMALLOWS	HOT CHOCOLATE
KETCHUP	FRIDAY	GRANDMA	BEAK
ICE CREAM	CHANNEL	RYE	BASKETBALL
TONGUE	SIGHT	WAITERS	SAW
FOGGY	CUSTODIAN	PLASTER	TRANSMISSION
PHOTOS	BROWNIES	LEASH	WAGON

Answers will vary.

Categorization (Page 170)

HORSE	START *	NUMBER
PENNY	SYCAMORE	COUNTRY
CIRCLE	GRANITE	RIVER
FOOT	QUARTER	MAP
LOS ANGELES	NOSE	UMBRELLA
PANTS	ALLIGATOR	CARNATION
SOUTH	HAWAII	PIANO
YARD	ORANGE	PURPLE
SOIL	GOALIE	YEAR
TANGO	MOTORCYCLE	LEAF
SNOW	PIZZA	VIOLIN
BALLET	TORNADO	DRIBBLE
ENCYCLOPEDIA	COOKIE	GLOSSARY
ELECTION	SAND	MILK
BANANA	FINISH *	MOUSE

Answers will vary. Possible answers include:
horse—cow, goat
piano—guitar, flute
purple—blue, yellow
banana—apple, strawberry

Fact or Opinion? (Page 175)

CHILDREN UNDER THE AGE OF SIXTEEN SHOULDN'T BE ALLOWED TO SKI.	FINISH * RAINBOWS ARE MORE BEAUTIFUL THAN SUNSETS.	THE INTERNET IS AVAILABLE AROUND THE WORLD.
BATS ARE SCARY.	EVERY PARENT SHOULD KNOW HOW TO SEW.	MANY SCHOOLS DO NOT ALLOW BUBBLE GUM CHEWING ON CAMPUS.
THE CITY IS TOO CROWDED.	MANY SPECIES IN THE RAINFOREST ARE ENDANGERED.	VACATIONS ON CRUISE SHIPS ARE THE MOST LUXURIOUS.
TURTLES LOOK VERY OLD.	A TOUCHDOWN SCORES SIX POINTS IN FOOTBALL.	BEES ARE ANGRY INSECTS.
THAT SHOW IS THE BEST!	YOU SHOULD PLAY ON THE BASEBALL TEAM.	THE TEAM WITH THE MOST GOALS IN THE SOCCER GAME WINS.
EVERY CHILD LOVES TO EAT PIZZA.	MANY TEENAGERS HAVE CELL PHONES.	SCHOOL PREPARES YOU FOR YOUR FUTURE.
DRINKING BOTTLED WATER IS BETTER FOR YOUR BODY.	MULTIPLICATION IS A SKILL LEARNED IN MATH.	HAMSTERS ARE CUTE AND CUDDLY.
NEEDLES ARE USED TO SEW.	SNAKES ARE CREEPY AND SLIMY.	ICE CREAM IS BEST BETWEEN TWO COOKIES.
BATS ARE NOCTURNAL ANIMALS.	EVERY CHILD LOVES CHEWING BUBBLE GUM.	CRUISE SHIPS CARRY PEOPLE ON VACATIONS ALL OVER THE WORLD.
A PERSON CAN NEVER HAVE TOO MANY FISH IN AN AQUARIUM.	THE PURPOSE OF HOMEWORK IS TO HELP YOU PRACTICE AND LEARN.	IT IS UNSAFE TO DRINK OCEAN WATER.
HAMSTERS USE AN EXERCISE WHEEL.	MY TEAM WILL WIN THE NEXT SOCCER GAME.	BEES PRODUCE HONEY.
THE RAINFOREST IS THE SAFEST PLACE TO VACATION.	A PERSON NEEDS A BOAT TO WATER SKI.	MATH IS THE MOST DIFFICULT SUBJECT.
TURTLES MOVE VERY SLOWLY.	WE GO TO THE BEST SCHOOL IN OUR STATE.	A CITY IS USUALLY RUN BY A MAYOR.
OUR TEACHER ASSIGNS TOO MUCH HOMEWORK.	SNAKES ARE MEMBERS OF THE REPTILE FAMILY.	ALL THE FOOTBALL PLAYERS DO IS TACKLE EACH OTHER.
START *	ICE CREAM IS A DAIRY PRODUCT.	RAINBOWS ARE OFTEN VISIBLE AFTER A RAINSTORM.

1. fact—The Internet is available around the world.
2. opinion—That show is the best!
3. opinion—You should play on the basketball team.
4. opinion—Every child loves to eat pizza.
5. fact—Many teenagers have cell phones.

Vocabulary 1 (Page 180)

START →	ASTONISHED	CONTINUE	ORDINARY
SHELTER	SCHEDULE	INVENTED	COMPARED
CONTRASTED	CURIOUS	STUMBLED	ENCOURAGED
ERROR	VANISHED	CANISTER	WHIRLING
SOCIAL	GRADUALLY	ILLUSTRATIONS	CAPTIONS
PROCLAIMED	HARDSHIPS	PONDER	DARTED
GUILT	CLIMATE	CIRCULATED	OPPONENTS
FOE	ANCESTORS	FRETTED	KNOWLEDGE
ERRANDS	SKETCH	FOUNDED	ELDEST
ADMITTED	INSPECTING	RELEASED	TRAGIC
A	B	C	D

Sentences will vary.

Vocabulary 2 (Page 185)

T	E	M	P	O	R	A	R	Y	O	D	O	R	L	E	S	S	A	A
O	R	E	C	L	I	N	I	N	G	A	E	I	O	U	C	A	U	U
R	S	T	R	E	N	G	T	H	I	N	F	O	R	M	A	F	T	D
D	I	N	D	E	S	T	R	U	C	T	I	B	L	E	R	R	H	I
I	S	E	N	T	E	R	T	A	I	N	M	E	N	T	D	U	E	T
N	C	P	U	C	O	A	X	F	A	E	I	O	U	I	I	S	N	I
A	E	R	T	I	I	O	T	L	A	E	E	A	I	O	G	T	T	O
R	N	O	I	U	A	A	E	I	P	R	O	F	I	T	A	R	I	N
Y	T	M	L	S	D	U	R	N	U	U	O	I	A	E	N	A	C	E
S	E	P	I	E	R	D	R	C	T	E	X	T	U	R	E	T	U	I
C	D	T	Z	I	O	I	O	H	A	M	O	T	I	O	N	E	A	U
A	P	I	E	Z	W	T	R	P	E	N	A	L	T	Y	O	D	N	U
R	E	N	A	E	S	I	U	N	E	X	P	E	C	T	E	D	N	I
C	T	T	P	A	Y	O	E	I	N	A	R	R	A	T	O	R	U	N
E	I	E	P	A	E	N	I	O	U	U	A	I	E	N	V	Y	A	T
D	T	R	R	D	E	S	T	R	U	C	T	I	V	E	I	U	L	E
E	E	V	O	M	A	T	U	R	E	U	A	R	E	S	I	S	T	R
S	A	A	A	A	R	E	Q	U	E	S	T	O	A	E	I	O	U	I
C	I	L	C	I	O	A	T	T	E	M	P	T	O	U	I	E	A	O
E	O	S	H	F	O	R	E	C	A	S	T	E	I	O	U	U	E	R
N	U	U	A	O	P	R	E	C	I	O	U	S	D	E	T	E	S	T
D	C	A	U	T	I	O	U	S	O	A	F	L	E	X	I	B	L	E

Sentences will vary.

Vocabulary in Context 1 (Page 190)

START *	MEADOW	PASSAGE	FURIOUS	DELICATE
INTRODUCE	DIRECTIONS	ADMIT	CALCULATE	DISAPPOINTED
STROLL	GLANCE	GENEROUS	UNFAIR	PROUD
ARTIFICIAL	RECOGNIZE	COMPLIMENTS	GREEDY	IDENTICAL
IMMENSE	INTENSE	CONDOMINIUM	DISPOSE	DISCOUNT
DEPOSIT	PANIC	CONCLUSION	STATIONARY	VANISH
PREPARE	NAUGHTY	OBSTACLE	ATTEND	ADVERTISING
RESERVATION	PERMISSION	DENY	PRESCRIPTION	BOREDOM
CHAMPION	BRAVE	DOUBTFUL	REGISTRATION	EVIDENCE
EAGER	PENALTY	FINISH * COMBINE	DEFEND	COOPERATE

Sentences will vary.

Vocabulary in Context 2 (Page 195)

LIMITED	SUCCESSFUL	FINISH * MERCHANDISE	CHEF
PERSIST	DEMONSTRATE	MONITOR	FREQUENTLY
TALENT	IGNORE	DODGE	EXCEL
PERSUADE	CANCELLED	CARELESSLY	DEFECTIVE
EMPHASIZE	ACCURATE	SPACIOUS	EXAGGERATE
VARIETY	COMPROMISE	OBLIGATION	ENCOURAGE
MAINTAIN	TYPICAL	ESTIMATE	PURPOSE
REMIND	DISPLAY	FUTURE	ADVANCE
DEPENDABLE	COMPANION	PROCEED	REWARD
OPPORTUNITY	CONCENTRATE	DRAMATIC	PUBLIC
PROVIDE	BEHAVIOR	BARELY	START *

Sentences will vary.

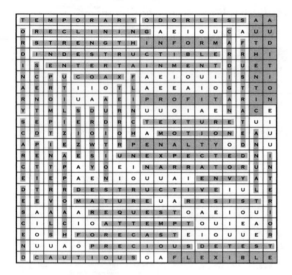

Notes